The Birth of The Chocolate City
Life in Georgian York

Summer Strevens

AMBERLEY

For Avril Goodwin, lover of all the sweet things in life.

First published 2014

Amberley Publishing
The Hill, Stroud
Gloucestershire, GL5 4EP

www.amberley-books.com

ISBN 978 1 4456 3346 6 (print)
ISBN 978 1 4456 3357 2 (ebook)

British Library Cataloguing in Publication Data.
A catalogue record for this book is available from the British Library.

Typesetting by Amberley Publishing.
Printed in the UK.

Contents

Acknowledgements

The research and writing of this book has been a fascinating, and at times a literally mouth-watering experience. In spite of my personal ingestion in the name of research, I would like to express my gratitude to a number of people without whose help and support, especially in the provision of images, this publication would have been much diminished.

Firstly, I would like to thank Ian Drake, keeper of the Evelyn Collection for the Yorkshire Architectural & York Archaeological Society, whose unwavering patience in the face of my requests for contemporary images of Georgian York was nothing but saintly. I would also like to express my gratitude to Alexandra Hutchinson, archivist and historian for Nestlé, who was happy to share with me her limitless knowledge of the history of the chocolate industry, chocolate manufacture, in fact everything chocolate! Grateful thanks are also due to Dr Amanda Jones, archivist with the Borthwick Institute and Bridget Morris, Director of The Rowntree Society; to Ralph Hewitt who is marketing anager at York's Chocolate Story, to Michael Woodward, York Museums Trust, to Brian Elsey creator of Historyworld.co.uk, a veritable treasure trove of vintage advertising, to the editorial team of Grace's Guide, a wonderful online repository of our industrial past, as well as Harry Drummond, whose dudleymall.co.uk is the world web centre for the Rayner family of artists.

Grateful mention should also be made of Mrs Heather Jones and her husband Deryck, and Miss Tor Jones (no relation). whose tirelessly energy and enthusiasm in accompanying me around the city on my quests for photogenic heritage shots was very much appreciated – literally keeping up with the Joneses!

Special commendation is also due to my publishers for their infinite encouragement, and finally I am eternally indebted to my long-suffering partner, Jack Gritton, without whose technical assistance and enduring patience and support I would have been lost.

To all those mentioned above, and everyone else who has given of their time, guided, advised and inspired, thank you.

INTRODUCTION

You might wonder – *another* book about chocolate in York? My first defence is, like consumption of the luscious wonder stuff itself, who can tire of chocolate?! Secondly, I wanted to examine the point of chocolate's 'birth' in York, and what kind of a city it was born into.

York is a city that takes a pride in its chocolate heritage. From Mary Tuke, the indisputable bedrock of York's Quaker chocolate origins in the eighteenth century, her humble grocers shop evolving into the iconic Rowntrees, to the opening of York's 'Chocolate Story' in the spring of 2012, the themed visitor attraction charting the history and rise of the city's prominent chocolate manufacturers and importance of confectionery to York.

I have chosen to focus on the Georgian period as this is the era in which the foundations for the later industry were firmly laid. Spanning the reigns of the first four Hanoverian Georges and William IV, butting up to the eponyms Victorian age, it was a time of immense social change in Britain, with the beginnings of the Industrial Revolution. However, as we shall see, York's exclusion from an emerging economy dominated by industry and machine manufacture would be one of the determining factors in the birth of the 'Chocolate City'.

A great tradition that continues to this day, there are echoes of York's chocolate past to be found all over the city, yet no account of York and the importance that chocolate has played in the city's economic history would be complete without first giving an introduction to the provenance and wonder of chocolate itself ...

The burnished, dark-brown, appetisingly bitter and chemically complex chocolate we enjoy today bears little resemblance to the pulp-enveloped seeds of the cocoa tree from which it is derived. From its earliest pre-Columbian roots, the ancient Mayans described chocolate as 'food of the gods' and were probably the first to cultivate the cacao tree from around AD 600. Imbibed as an unsweetened drink that the Maya called *xocoatle*, and flavoured with vanilla or spiked with chili, cocoa beans were a valuable commodity and were even used as currency. Later, the Aztecs continued to enjoy and economically prize chocolate, with the infamous Montezuma, Aztec emperor at the time of the Conquistadors' arrival even establishing a bean bank accepting tribute in cacao beans and trading with them in the absence of any coin-based currency. Montezuma himself is reputed to have drunk upwards of fifty cups of chocolate a day in the commonly held belief that it was an aphrodisiac, and with two wives, nine daughters, eleven sons and many, many concubines, clearly his virility cannot be called into question.

Chocolate's later introduction to Europe in the sixteenth century was a consequence of Hernan Cortes and the Spanish Conquistadores' search for El Dorado; though gold was their ultimate goal, they also stumbled upon a commodity that would become ubiquitous in the western world as the smooth, melt-in-the-mouth, heavenly product so many of us crave today. The desire for chocolate has even spawned the descriptive term 'chocoholic', a phrase first coined in 1961 when a journalist from the *Pasadena Independent* asked 'Would you call a person who is over fond of chocolates a chocoholic?'

Of course, pleasure has long been paralleled with the state of sin, and Devil's Food Cake aside, it has even been mooted that Willy Wonka of Roald Dahl's *Charlie & The Chocolate Factory* fame is the personification of Satan himself, with his ultimate arsenal of taste temptations...

Post-Montezuma's prolific prowess, chocolate's associations with the erotic has proliferated through the ages; Giacomo Casanova found chocolate to be as good an icebreaker with the ladies as was champagne. Louis XV's exquisite *maîtresse-en-titre*, Madame de Pompadour, reputedly employed chocolate to liven up her own lacklustre passions, her prevalent attitude to sex one of frigidity, and in order to 'stir up a sensuality that was at best sluggish' she exploited the alleged aphrodisiac properties of chocolate. Conversely, the Pompadour's successor, Madame du Barry, was accused of using chocolate to excite her lovers in an endeavour to satisfy her own rapacious sexual desires. The notorious Marquis de Sade was also a fan of chocolate, an essential refreshment served at his saturnalian parties, from his prison cell de Sade remonstrated with his long-suffering Marquise that the chocolate sponge cake she had sent him did not contain enough chocolate, complaining that inside it should have been 'as black as the devil's arse is black from smoke'. Who better then, in the face of chocolate's carnal connotations, than the Quakers to reform the image of chocolate to that of a tool of the temperance movement?

As we shall see, the Quakers have had a longstanding association with the city, since George Fox, the founder of the Society of Friends, was unceremoniously thrown down the steps of York Minster in 1651 for preaching against the established church. However, Quakerism was just one of the collaborative influences that were the catalyst toward confectionery capitalisation. In spite of York's former economic decline, the city yet possessed the qualities that would make it such a fashionable destination in the Georgian 'age of elegance', a social and economic climate in which the seeds of the chocolate industry would grow and flourish, ripening into the three indisputably household names of Rowntree, Terry's and Craven, the stories of which, along with the history of the city that made this possible, I hope to tell with a chocolatey seam running throughout...

Onward then to the emergence of York as a city that today boasts the daily production of 6 million KitKats – that's over 1 billion a year – and in the words of National Chocolate Week: 'Sssh! Don't tell the dentist!'

1

Emerging 'Chocolate City': In the Beginning...

Once touted as an alternative capital for the Kingdom, the Roman colonia of *Eboracum* established between the rivers Ouse and Foss today is one of England's finest and most beautiful historic cities. Through the ages, falling to the Viking invader Ivar the Boneless and becoming the capital of the Scandinavian kingdom of 'Jorvik', York was later ravaged by a vengeful William the Conqueror in 1086 during his 'Harrying of the North'. However, by the early thirteenth century, the wealthy city's merchants were granted control of their own affairs and trade flourished; the essence of medieval York can still be explored through the evocative narrow streets and snickelways winding haphazardly through the city. York Minster, built over two centuries and designed to be the greatest cathedral in the kingdom became the city's glorious centrepiece and the city itself prospered. That is until the Civil War dealt a decisive blow to Royalist York's fabric and economy. Surrendering to the parliamentary army after the Siege of York in 1644, badly damaged, the city's prominent role in national life began to decline. While remaining the administrative capital of the Yorkshire Ridings, by the eighteenth century York was no longer a city of truly national importance, yet the Georgian period was nonetheless one of social and cultural growth for York. In the age of politeness and sophistication, the city developed into the social capital of the north, a magnet to the wealthy classes who came to regard York as an alternative to London. Assemblies, the theatre and the races were all part of an evolved social scene, and it was during this transformation that the foundations for the latter chocolate empires were laid.

But before we plunge into York's progression towards an entity of Georgian elegance, and the consequent underpinnings of the city's confectionery prominence, we should perhaps take a closer look at how and when chocolate first reached our shores in order to better appreciate its economic importance and growing social popularity, and consequent impact as an industry to York itself.

When Hernan Cortes and fellow Spanish Conquistadores scoured South America in the early sixteenth century in search of El Dorado, their repeated expeditions plundering the native Inca and Aztec empires failed to uncover the location of the mythical city of gold, but while the ultimate glittering prize eluded them, they did return bearing another treasure: the beans of the cacao tree. Already highly valued by the indigenous inhabitants of the Amazon basin, where the cocoa trees grew wild and flourished in the tropical rainforests, the cocoa bean was used as currency as well as the ingredient for a special chocolate drink. While Christopher Columbus is said to have been the first person to return to Spain with the cocoa

Botanical illustration of Theobroma cacao.

bean in 1492, when he presented the almond-shaped brown beans to his sponsors, the Catholic monarchs King Ferdinand and Queen Isabella, the other bounties disgorged from his galleons somewhat overshadowed the seemingly unassuming seeds of the cocoa tree. It wasn't until his fourth voyage to the New World between 1502 and 1504, alighting in what we now call Nicaragua, that Columbus discovered the cocoa bean being used as currency and made into a beverage, however, more intent on the primary goal of his voyage, namely to find the route to India in order to trade for spices, he still failed to recognise any potential market for cocoa. Latterly, it was Hernan Cortes, set on the conquest of the Aztec Empire, who was astute enough to recognise the bean's real commercial promise, and responsible for introducing chocolate to Europe via the Spanish Court of Charles V in 1528.

Postulating that if the resultant bitter beverage were blended with sugar it could become quite palatable, a delicacy even, on mixing the beverage with other exotic commodities such as vanilla, nutmeg, cloves, allspice and cinnamon, the Spaniards created a tantalising taste that was coveted by and reserved for the fashionable Spanish nobility, the secret of which Spain managed to keep from the rest of the globe for almost a hundred years.

But the taste for exotic chocolate spread to France when, in 1615, Louis XIII's Spanish bride the Infanta Anne introduced the inticing new drink to an eager French court, presenting her husband-to-be with an engagement gift of chocolate, elegantly packaged in an ornate chest. Chocolate proved extremely popular in France, and not only to the tastes of the succeeding Louis XIV and his entourage at the court of Versailles. The Sun King so enjoyed the drink that he appointed Sieur David Illou to develop chocolate for manufacture and sale, creating a craze for chocolate which took Paris by storm and soon spread throughout France.

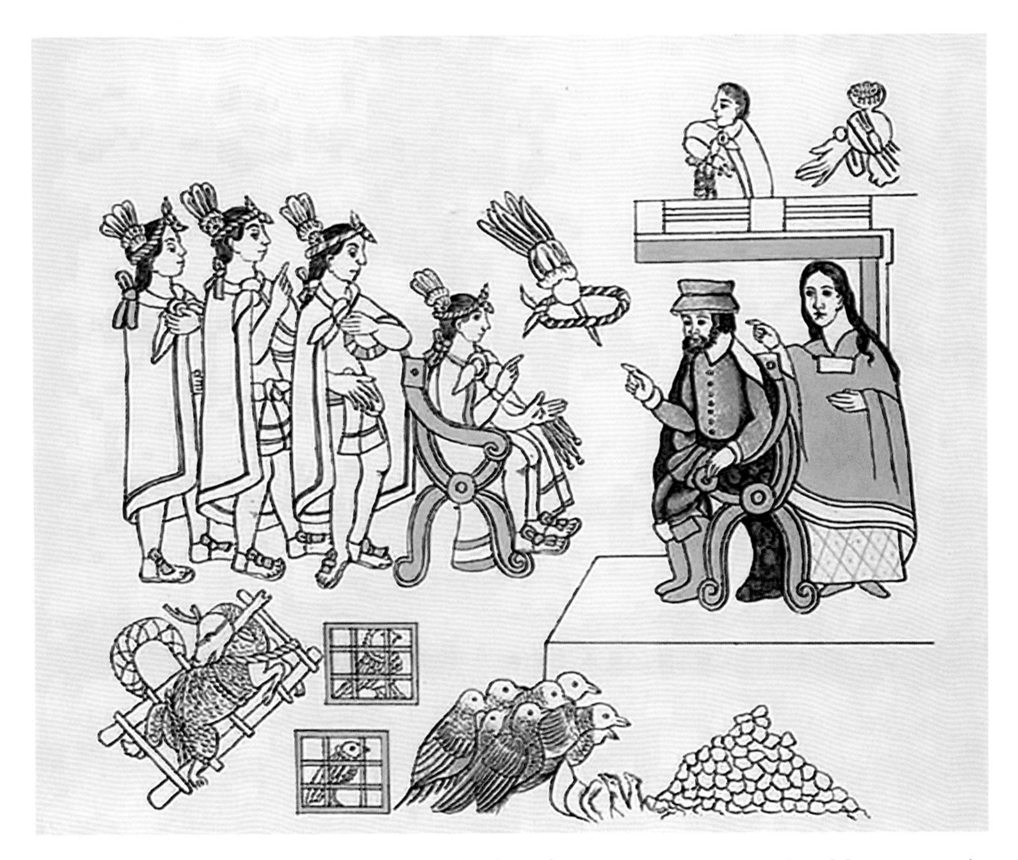

Hernan Cortes, conquistador and early chocolate impresario, meeting Montezuma in Tenochtitlan, 8 November 1519.

It took a while for the English and Dutch to show the same appreciation however; cocoa beans found on board captured Spanish 'treasure ships' were tossed overboard by English and Dutch crews reputedly assuming the cargo to be sheep dung! When chocolate finally reached England's shores in the 1650s, hastened by the capture of Spanish-controlled Jamaica in 1655, where cocoa plantations were well established, it became very popular at the court of Charles II. While at this stage a beverage accessible to only the very wealthy due to exorbitant import duties (at this time chocolate cost about 15*s* a pound, which would be equivalent to around £85 in today's money), chocolate did gradually become more readily accessible to the lower echelons of society, and by the mid-seventeenth century 'chocolate houses' had begun to emerge throughout Europe alongside the already well-established coffee houses. In 1657, a French shopkeeper opened the first 'chocolate house' in London, and in the *Publick Advertiser* printed Tuesday 16 June 1657, the first advertisement for chocolate announced that 'In Bishopgate St, in Queen's Head Alley, at a Frenchman's house, is an excellent West Indian drink called Chocolate to be sold, where you may have it ready at any time and also unmade at reasonable rates.'

Celebrated diarist Samuel Pepys, whose private and coded entries were made between 1660 and 1669 and give an invaluable glimpse into post-restoration life, penned numerous entries pertaining to chocolate and 'Jocolatte', now an available beverage clearly part of daily life and society. Pepys even employed 'Jocolatte' as a hangover cure; after a heavy

Engraving of a scene from a seventeenth-century Chocolate House.

night on the town celebrating Charles II's Coronation, his diary entry for Wednesday 24 April 1661 ran, 'Waked in the morning with my head in a sad taking through the last night's drink, which I am very sorry for; so rose and went out with Mr. Creed to drink our morning draft, which he did give me in chocolate to settle my stomach'. Early next century, Dr Johnson, famed for his *A Dictionary of the English Language*, would employ chocolate as a brake on his alcohol consumption, taking 'his chocolate liberally, pouring in large quantities of cream, or even melted butter' (around 1700, the English decided to improve the drink by adding milk). The portrait of Johnson in his later years does show a somewhat jowly, rotund gentleman, and while chocolate may have curbed his drinking, with the indulgent dairy additions it certainly did nothing for his waistline!

By the 1680s, chocolate houses were competing with the already popular and established coffee houses as an alternative place to dine, as well as venues in which to play at cards and dice and to gamble in general. Gambling in all forms seemed to be endemic and class-wide in the late Stuart era, a trend that carried through to the succeeding Georgian period. If a deck of cards was not to hand, something else could always be found to wager on, even if it concerned a race between two raindrops to see which would first reach the bottom of a window pane.

As with 'coffee house society', chocolate houses also provided the same climate and surroundings conducive to discourse and the discussion of current affairs, and it dawned upon astute chocolate house proprietors that their establishments could be exploited to present a wider business opportunity. Catering specifically to the rich and privileged male clientele, the 'gentleman's club' was born. The most famous of these was originally established at No. 4 Chesterfield Street in 1693, off Curzon Street in Mayfair, by an Italian immigrant named Francis White – Francesco Bianco to his countrymen – who opened a hot chocolate emporium under the name 'Mrs White's Chocolate House'. White's quickly made the transition to exclusive club and was notorious as a gambling house, and in 1778 it moved to the fashionable St James's Street address that is still occupied by this exclusive gentlemen's club today.

London, however, did not have the monopoly on fashion and taste. York during the Georgian era was the acknowledged premiere northern magnet for those with riches and privilege at a remove from the capital. The prominent and affluent flocked to the *Eboracorum* described by Drake in his *The History and Antiquities of the City of York* as 'no place, out of London, so polite and elegant to live in as the city of York'.

Long acknowledged as the 'second city', York was the capital of a substantial regional entity. The city's role as a diocesan and county centre, home to prominent religious and secular institutions, particularly the minster and court assizes, was already well established. However, in the eighteenth century, while Britain was Europe's forerunner in urban development, York had failed to share in the climate of growing commercial and industrial strengths, and the boom experienced in the rise of industrial and port towns like Manchester, Birmingham, Liverpool and Glasgow rather passed York by.

Consequently, York's emergence as a city of Georgian elegance, drawing the well-heeled from the surrounding country, and in turn generating business on many levels, was a situation to be encouraged by the City Fathers in the face of York's ongoing socio-economic decline.

In the past, the city's location on the River Ouse and proximity to the Great North Road had assured York's position as a major trading centre in medieval times. A major cloth manufacturing centre, in the later Middle Ages York merchants were importing wine from

The era of urban and industrial development rather passed York by, as reflected in this somewhat pastoral view of the city in the eighteenth century. (*Engraving by William Miller*)

France, and cloth, wax, canvas and oats from the Low Countries, as well as timber and furs from the Baltic. On the export front, grain was shipped to Gascony and the Low Countries, the latter also large importers of English wool. However, the Tudor period saw York enter an economic decline, precipitated by the Dissolution of the Monasteries ending the existence of many of the large and prominent monastic institutions crucial to the city's economy, and reducing York's role to that of a trading and service centre. As mentioned earlier, in 1644, during the Civil War, York's fabric was further decimated when the city was besieged by the Parliamentarians. Further decline occurred after the Restoration of the monarchy in 1660, as with an increase in national stability, the role of the military garrison at York Castle was being called into question by the 1680s, and following the removal of the Royal Garrison from York in 1688 this had a detrimental financial impact, as did the silting up of the River Ouse, which resulted in York losing its pre-eminent position as a trading centre to the port of Hull. (By the early nineteenth century, dredging and other improvements to the river Foss had the knock-on effect of making it impossible to import flour into York by river, thereby reducing the economic significance of the Castle Mills). Competition from other nearby cities like Leeds and Bradford further compounded the decline in the city's fortunes, consequently leading to an economic diametric reliant on the local gentry and merchants, thus encouraging and spawning the sophisticated consumer economy that was to grow and support York throughout the Georgian era.

There is little doubt that the City Corporation would have had in mind a strategy for refashioning and elevating the profile of the city to better fit with the perceived paradigms of civility, sociability and politeness of the times – core requirements in forming the backbone of York's economic future success as a the 'social capital' of the North. Probably the most cosmetically prominent vestiges of this striving toward the fashionable Georgian ethos can be found in the surviving examples of the *à la mode* architecture of the period. After all, architecture itself is a major aspect of conspicuous consumption, and one architect in particular made a small fortune from the urban industry that arose from the design, construction and modification to the fabric of the City of York.

John Carr (1723–1807) rose to prominence by capitalising on the creation of a range of recreational facilities patronised by the fashionable elite (and those aspiring as such), as well as elegant homes for them to live in. With an excellent grasp of geometry and proportion and an eye for detail, Carr paid meticulous attention to every stage of construction, with the result that the hallmark 'Carr of York' can be applied to some of the city's finest buildings: Castlegate House (across the way from Fairfax House, the interior of which was Carr's design); Bootham Park Hospital (formerly the county lunatic asylum) and the County Court House to name but three fine examples.

The need to cater to this emerging sophisticated consumer economy was also reflected in the construction of the stylish York Assembly Rooms, designed by Lord Burlington in the increasingly fashionable neo-palladian style. Opened in 1732, this venue for hosting high-class social gatherings has been described as one of the most influential pieces of architecture of the early eighteenth century. The Assembly Rooms were situated close to another new and stylish edifice, the Mansion House, home to the Lord Mayors of York, completed the same year (though the foundation stone had been laid in 1725, it took seven years to complete the building).

In 1730, the York Corporation took a further step in encouraging Georgian high society's love of 'promenading' with the construction of the New Walk alongside the River Ouse, a pedestrian avenue bordered by the dappled shade of lime and elm trees. The following year York Race Course was moved to the greatly improved site on the

Carr's County Court House. Many of Carr's private houses can still be admired in York today, including some classic façades on Bootham and Micklegate. Unfortunately Carr's own house on Skeldergate was demolished in 1945.

View of the Mansion House looking down Coney Street. (*Courtesy of The Evelyn Collection*)

Thomas Rowlandson's 'A Race on the Knavesmire at York'.

Knavesmire that is still occupies today (sadly Carr's impressive new grandstand built to accommodate the spectators is gone), with York Races being timed to follow the assizes in August, the better to monopolise on the presence of the landed gentry, who travelled to town for court business. It was noted in 1714 that 'such was the concourse of nobility and gentry that attended York races that one hundred and fifty coaches were at one time on the course'.

Capitalising on the Georgian love of drama and performance, in 1744 the curtain was raised on the stage of the New Theatre, later taken over by Tate Wilkinson and granted a Royal Patent in 1769. Renamed the Theatre Royal, in its Georgian heyday the York stage attracted many of the finest actors of the period, including John Philip Kemble and his sister Sarah Siddons, Dorothea Jordan and Elizabeth Farren.

Catering then to the new market opportunities of this increasingly sophisticated consumer economy, the growth in the number of service industries, of luxury craftsmen and in the retail sector was a direct response to the burgeoning demands of the gentrified classes; goldsmiths and gunsmiths, clockmakers, booksellers, periwig makers, silk merchants, grocers and vintners all flourished, all appealing to the latest tastes among the wealthy, and of course there was an increase in the number of chocolate and coffee house in the city as well.

As the past hindrances of the politico-economic systems enforced by York's medieval trade guilds, which had proved so suffocating to developing trade, were now on the wane, increasing freedom to exploit this new dynamic element of the city's economy meant that new markets emerged too, namely what we would recognise as an early tourist industry. Travel for pleasure or health benefits in Britain and Ireland had become widely available to the affluent middling classes in the eighteenth century, and as opportunities for European travel had been severely

The fashionably 'romantic' ruins of St Mary's Abbey in York. (*Courtesy of the Yale Center for British Art, Paul Mellon Collection*)

hampered for much of the Georgian period, owing to the fact that Britain was perennially at war with at least one of its continental neighbours, the domestic tourist scene flourished. With a rising interest in antiquity, the pleasures of the picturesque fed by the 'gothic' fervour so ardently expressed in the literature of the period, and the taste for the fashionable mock architecture and folly meant that the once untoward ruins and timeworn medieval buildings abundant in York became objects of elitist appreciation. The promotion of these historic edifices helped develop an identity that would further assist in boosting York's flagging economy, helping to assure the city's survival as a centre of sociability and consequent consumption.

But what part did chocolate play in this new, polished society? As the discerning Georgian consumer generated a positive economy in York, during the eighteenth century imported foodstuffs came to play a central role in everyday life. Alongside a demand for tea, politely sipped from fine china cups, and for snuff taken by smart gents strolling to the coffee houses, guests invited to the wealthier table would dine on dishes sweet and savoury that were laced with expensive spices and sugar. And of course chocolate was an essential luxury commodity, consumed along with those other purchases that filled the tea caddies, spice caskets, sugar bowls and pepper boxes of the privileged York gentry. At this time, chocolate would have been available to buy in solid blocks of grainy cocoa, a hardened chocolate paste in all likelihood processed in Jamaica and imported from Spain, although as a sideline, chocolate houses also sold a pressed cake form for those wanting to make the drink at home, dissolved in milk or water to produce a foamy chocolate drink.

Earlier recipes did exist for the processing of the raw bean itself. In 1672, William Hughes published details of how to do this:

> Take as many of the cacao's as you have a desire to make up at one time, and put as many of them at once into a frying-pan (being very clean scoured) as will cover the bottom thereof, and hold them over a moderate fire, shaking them so, that they may not burn (for you must have a very great care of that) until they are dry enough to peel off the outward crust skin; and after they are dried and peeled then beat them in an iron mortar, until it will rowl [sic] up into great balls or rows and be sure you beat it not over-much neither, for then it will become too much oyly.

While in Hannah Woolley's *The Queen-Like Closet,* published in 1670 (an early household management book), her recipe is clearly working with the block form of cocoa. She instructs,

> Take half a pint of Clarret Wine, boil it a little, then scrape some Chaculato very fine and put into it, and the Yokes of two Eggs, stir them well together over a slow Fire till it be thick, and sweeten it with Sugar according in your taste.

Chocolate was also regarded as medicinally beneficial, and as mentioned in the introduction even carried a reputation as something of an aphrodisiac. Purported to be an effective treatment in a wide variety of disorders from stomach and intestinal complaints,

Hannah Woolley from the frontispiece of *The Gentlewoman's Companion*, or, *A Guide to the Female Sex*, published 1673.

childhood diarrhoea, reduction of fevers, expulsion of phlegm and beneficial to those suffering from 'female complaints', incredibly chocolate was also said to be efficacious in delaying hair growth! In 1741, Swedish naturalist Carl Linnaeus mentions rather candidly in his monograph on chocolate that through drinking chocolate he cured himself of haemorrhoids.

Clearly, the curative regard in which chocolate was held accounts for the fact that some of the earliest cocoa makers were apothecaries (early chemists), intrigued by the supposed medicinal properties it held. Possessing the necessary skills and equipment to measure, heat and blend components and ingredients used in the then everyday remedies and preparations, it comes as no surprise that such skills would be utilised in the early production of chocolate. In fact, two household names in chocolate production have their origins in the apothecary business, namely Fry's of Bristol and the home-grown Terry's of York, although, as we shall see, the path to later chocolate production on a massive commercial scale also led from the grocer's shop. At the emergence then of York as 'Chocolate City', while there were many confectioners involved in small scale production in the city, there were three burgeoning enterprises that would later come to dominate the confectionary scene.

As the next chapter of this book attests, it was Mary Tuke who was indeed the 'mother' of York's chocolate industry – her life and achievements warranting a separate and comprehensive retelling, as it was her grocery shop opened in Walmgate in 1725 that was indubitably the foundation stone upon which the later Rowntree chocolate empire was to stand. The fortitude of this Quaker businesswoman, who successfully rebelled against the trading restrictions of the Merchant Adventurers Company, assured the continuation of her grocery business to successive generations of her family, later evolving into the Rowntree empire that was so impactful, economically and socially, on York itself.

Of course, the familial legacy of the Rowntrees themselves has an integral place in the emergence of York as the 'Chocolate City'. In 1822, while Tukes was still a family concern, now entering a fourth generation, Samuel Tuke's good friend of Joseph Rowntree I, a fellow Quaker who also hailed from a grocery background (the young Joseph had worked in his father's grocery shop in Scarborough since the age of eleven), was now an independent grocer, having just purchased, on his twenty-first birthday, his own shop at No. 28 Pavement in the city. The auctioning of the premises at the Elephant & Castle Inn on Skeldergate was a somewhat colorful affair, and the auctioneer was so drunk that Joseph had to plunge his head into a bucket of cold water before he could proceed with the sale! In 1832, Joseph married Sarah Stephenson after a courtship suppressed and lengthened on Joseph's part, in deference to the bereavement suffered by Sarah when her father died in 1828. A family soon followed, the eldest child, John Stephenson, born in 1834, was followed in 1836 by Joseph, and Henry Isaac in 1838, Hannah Elizabeth in 1840, and finally Sarah Jane (known in the family as Sally), in 1843, sadly this last daughter succombed to whooping cough and died aged five years.

The business in Pavement prospered and, in 1845, the Rowntree family moved to Blossom Street, and then again in 1848 to No. 39 Bootham (both locations had been within the catchment of those elegant townhouses to have appeared in the earlier Georgian era).

During the 1850s, Joseph's two elder sons both became partners in the grocery business, but it was Joseph's youngest son, Henry Isaac Rowntree, who would later buy the Tukes chocolate and cocoa business – Terry's of York and M. A. Craven & Son, (more of the Rowntree meteoric rise to the status of 'chocolate giant' will be examined in a later chapter, as we turn our attention to the other prodigious names who emerged in the Georgian York, further underpinning the city's confectionary history).

Joseph Rowntree's house at No. 49 Bootham.

Eighteenth-century Bootham Bar as it would have appeared when Robert Berry set up shop. (*Courtesy of The Evelyn Collection*)

While Mary Tuke's family business was evolving under the management of her nephew, in 1767, on the other side of the city, the origins of another chocolate eminence was developing. In that year, Robert Berry opened a shop close to Bootham Bar selling cough lozenges, lemon and orange candied peel and other sweets.

Joined by William Bayldon, the partners renamed the business Bayldon & Berry Confectionery. Bayldon and Berry continued together in the confectionary business until, as reported in the *London Gazette* of 1 March 1821, 'The Partnership carried on by us, William Bayldon and Robert Berry, as Confectioners, at the City of York, under the firm of Bayldon and Berry, is dissolved by mutual consent.' While Berry continued the concern without his partner, in another part of the city, a young man named Joseph Terry was busy building his own business.

Born in 1793 to a farming family in Pocklington on the outskirts York, Joseph Terry came to Stonegate in the city to serve his seven-year apprenticeship training as an apothecary.

Having acquired the skills to compound pharmacopoeia preparations, to recognise drugs and their use, and to dispense complicated prescriptions from medicines mostly derived from herbs, plants and vegetables, on successfully gaining his certificates, Joseph set up in his own chemist shop. An advertisement in the *York Courant* (York's earliest newspaper) in 1813 announced he had established his own business located 'opposite the Castle, selling spices, pickling vinegar, essence of spruce, patent medicines and perfumery'. It may appear that some of the items listed cross over into the realm of the grocer's shop, but as early as the twelfth century apothecaries had belonged to the Worshipful Company of Grocers, a guild that included the pepperers and the spicers as well as apothecaries.

Joseph later moved his business to premises in Walmgate, where customers could also purchase from the well-stocked 'leech jars', either to affect a home remedy, for say the swelling of a black eye, or alternatively Mr Terry could perform the service for you.

A sketch of late eighteenth-century Stonegate, as it would have appeared when Joseph Terry was serving his apothecary apprenticeship. (*Courtesy of The Evelyn Collection*)

However, in 1823, at the age of thirty, matrimony was to turn Joseph's fortunes in the direction of confectionery.

Marriage to Harriet Atkinson, sister-in-law to Robert Berry, brought Joseph into the sphere of that family's business, and on the death of Robert Berry, Joseph closed his chemist shop on Walmgate, and took over the running of firm, together with Berry's son George. An advert in the *Yorkshire Gazette* dated 29 October 1825, stated,

> Joseph Terry and George Berry, confectioners, St Helen's Square, having taken the Stock and entered upon the premises of the late Robert Berry and Co., most respectfully solicit from the Friends of the late Firm and from the Public at large that Patronage so liberally bestowed on their Predecessors.

The harmoniously renamed 'Berry & Terry' was a partnership that was short lived however, George Berry quitting the confectionery business in 1828. Now solely running the business from premises in St Helen's Square, and with a factory in Brearly Yard, Joseph expanded the range to include confits, medicated lozenges (a nod to his former profession), marmalade, mushroom ketchup and the forerunner of the modern 'love heart' sweets, saucy 'conversation lozenges' with teasing messages like 'how do you flirt?' inscribed on them; Joseph also renamed the company 'Terry's of York'.

The former Terry's of York premises in St Helen's Square, today occupied by crystal specialists Swarovski – the name 'TERRY' can still be seen in the stonework and beneath the shop window.

Terry's confectionery concern prospered. Advantageously located in the very heart of York, St Helen's Square, then as now, was filled with shoppers and tourists, their numbers augmenting with the rise of railway travel and the swelling capacity of trains carrying up to 30,000 passengers to York on the thirteen daily services that ran to the city (a staggering increase when one considers rail was fast replacing the two daily stagecoaches services accounting for 23,000 passengers a *year*).

Joseph Terry was also shrewd enough to realise that by utilising the rising North Eastern Railway network, York being its hub, this would enable Terry's to despatch small quantities of confectionery products to towns and cities all over the north of England, going on to expand an initially local Yorkshire distribution into the Midlands and out to London and beyond, eventually delivering to over seventy-five destinations all over England. Consequently, by the time Joseph died in 1850, the name of Terry's of York was a recognisable brand throughout Britain, a distinctive heritage that his son and successor, Joseph Junior, expanded into a major concern, the rise and ultimate decline of which will be discussed in 'Chocolate City Then and Now'.

The third confectionery business to have a significant impact on the development of 'Chocolate City', with its roots firmly planted in the Georgian era, was Cravens. Manufacturers of quality sugar confectionery, Craven's would go on to be at one time the world's largest boiled sweet manufacturer. The origins of M. A. Craven & Son lay with

Folio 147

ESTABLISHED 1822.

M. A. Craven & Son, LIMITED.

Ebor Confectionery Works,

YORK, 6 - JUL 1916 191

Messrs W. Parkinson & Son,
Grocers,
Thornton Dale.

EBOR TRADE MARK.

CODES USED: A.B.C. & WESTERN UNION.
TELEGRAMS: "CRAVEN, YORK."

TELEPHONE 35.

1916		£	s.	d.	£	s.	d.
June 7	To Goods	1	15	10			
16	By Empts					7	4
			7	4			
					£ 1	8	6

15937

EBOR CONFECTIONERY WORKS,

York, July 6 1916

Received from W. Parkinson

the sum of One Pounds,

Eight Shillings, Six Pence.

For M. A. CRAVEN & SON. Ltd.

Cash ... 1 : 8 : 6
Discount ... : :
Allowances : :
Amt. of A/c. 1 : 8 : 6

J. D. Smith

Invoice issued by M. A. Craven & Son from the Ebor Confectionery Works, dated 6 July 1916.

twenty-nine-year-old Joseph Hick, who set up in business as a confectioner in York in partnership with Richard Kilner in 1803. However, as detailed in the *London Gazette*:

> Notice is hereby given, that the copartnership heretofore subsisting between Richard Kilner and Joseph Hick, of the City of York, Confectioners, under the firm of Kilner and Hick, was dissolved by mutual consent on the 5th day of May last: As witness our hands this 16th day of November 1822.
>
> Rich. Kilner.
> Joseph Hick.

The partnership at an end, Hick relocated the business to No. 47 Coney Street. Today Coney Street is one of York's main shopping thoroughfares populated by many familiar high street retailers. In Hick's day the premises neighboured the Leopard Inn, opposite St Martin's church; his had had a decent footfall of potential customers. Seven years later, Hick's youngest daughter, Mary Ann, was born, and it was she who would later form M. A. Craven & Son Ltd.

Into the story now steps Thomas Craven. Arriving in York in 1833, a farmer's son from the East Riding, he was apprenticed to his brother-in-law Thomas Hide, who had established a confectionery business in York in the mid-1820s at No. 20 High Ousegate. However, by 1843, Craven appears to have been established in his own premises, the *York Courant* on 26 October that year describing him as a purveyor of 'confectionery, teas, coffees etc'. On 1 May 1845, Craven had moved his business to No. 31 Pavement, not far from the Rowntree's shop. Now a self-made man, the thirty-four-year-old Craven took the twenty-two-year-old Mary Ann Hick as his wife on 30 April 1851. The business must have been doing well as at the time of his marriage, Thomas Craven was prosperous enough to buy the Pavement building outright for £1,300, in addition to a further site at No. 10 Castlegate, his employees at this time numbering sixty-three men and sixty boys.

On 20 February 1860, Mary Ann's father died, his estate and the Coney Street confectionery business was divided between his three children. Then, in 1862, Thomas Craven died, leaving the thirty-three year old Mary Ann to manage the upbringing of their three children and the running of both confectionery businesses. Her initial and understandable reaction was to try to sell both concerns, however delay caused by the negligence of her solicitors and consequent overbearing financial burdens led Mary Ann to make the decision to merge both concerns in an attempt to sustain a livelihood, trading under the name M. A. Craven, her son Joseph William joining the company in 1881, hence the '& Son'.

A lady of apparently short stature – she would sit on a high chair the better to oversee production – Mary Ann went on to run the company for more than forty years, right up until her own death in 1902. Production centred on the Coppergate site, where the Jorvik Viking Centre stands today, and was known as the Ebor Confectionery Works (also known as the French Almond Works), manufacture of sugared almonds, pastilles, gums, mints, boiled sweets, toffees and nougat were the primary concern.

In addition, there were also four retail shops in the city stocking and selling Craven's confections, and the one in the Shambles, Craven's Mary Ann Sweet Shop, included on the first floor a confectionery museum.

From their modest beginnings then as embryonic businesses in the flourishing climate of York's Georgian opulence, Tuke's, Rowntree's, Terry's and Craven's were family confectionery concerns that all adhered to the same principles of excellence and quality, assuring their later status as household names synonymous with York's confectionery industry and history.

2

Mother of York's Chocolate Industry: Mary Tuke

If we are to examine the true circumstances surrounding the 'birth' of York as 'Chocolate City', we must trace the conception of commercial confection back to the year 1725, to a remarkable woman who was the earliest strand woven into the tapestry of York's confectionary empires.

Mary Tuke was a thirty-year-old spinster when she took the decision to open her own grocery shop in Walmgate in the city. Her mother, Rebecka, had died two years previously, and she was now head of the Tuke household, her father William having passed away in 1704.

In 1725, the York in which Mary set up shop was, though still the premiere city of the north, actually declining in commercial importance in the ever-increasing shadow of the other rapidly emerging industrial centres, like the growing mill towns of Lancashire and textile centres of Leeds, Bradford and Halifax. Nevertheless, York was still quite large, proportionally a market town rather than an industrial centre, and home to a diverse range of traditional trades such as butchers, bakers, brewers and coopers, tailors and shoemakers, comb makers and pipe makers – the tobacco variety that is. And of course York was the seat of ecclesiastic primacy for the north of England, the splendour of the Minster indicative of the office of Archbishop of York as the second highest prelate in the land, though this divine designation would have little bearing on Mary's religious concerns as she was a part of the Quaker community that had developed into the York Friends.

Outside of the city walls, the open countryside was giving way to 'modern' houses, elegant residences with tall brick façades punctuated by sash windows and smart front doors beneath a fashionable fanlight. Yet ancient overhanging timber-framed dwellings still proliferated within York's walls, set to a medieval street pattern, a flavour of which can still be tasted in The Shambles today. A tourist haven where some of the buildings date back to the fourteenth century, this street of butchers would have been familiar and little changed in Mary's time too, a number of the shops still retaining the metal meat hooks hanging outside and wooden shelves or 'shamels' beneath on which flesh for sale was displayed and from which the street took its name.

The London stagecoach would have rumbled into the old city beneath Micklegate Bar, which, though in dire need of structural repair still retained its barbican, like Walmgate's today. (Micklegate's crumbling barbican was eventually demolished in 1826). After a twenty-nine and a half hour journey, the High Flyer or the Wellington arrived from London carrying weary passengers, who disembarked into a city of medieval streets mingled with

Above: Blossom Street looking toward Micklegate, the emerging new classical façades juxtaposed with older frontages. (*Courtesy of The Evelyn Collection*)

Right: The Shambles today, one of the best-preserved medieval shopping streets in Europe.

some of the recently added Georgian façades, brooded over by the towering Minster. Itinerant tradesmen calling for custom – knives to grind or milk fresh from the cow – gossips, beggars, shoppers and tradesmen added to the din of market carts lumbering over the busy uneven roads, although congestion and rough carriageways would later be ameliorated by a special Act of Parliament imposing a five shilling fine on anyone leaving a waggon or carriage unattended.

Among this mixture of medieval gables and burgeoning Georgian terraces then, Mary Tuke's grocery shop on Walmgate began to trade. Specialising in tea, coffee and cocoa, the latter of which the privileged inhabitants of Bootham and Micklegate would have been served at breakfast from an elegant pot, like those of the local creamware manufactured in Leeds, Tuke's would also have carried the everyday commodities that would have been the grocer's stock in trade.

While Walmgate was never regarded as one of the smarter parts of town, when Tuke's opened it was respectable enough.

Old Micklegate Bar, prior to 1826, showing the crumbling barbican still in place.

Louise Rayner's painting of Walmgate. (*Courtesy of Harry Drummond, dudleymall.co.uk*)

However, by the end of the era covered by this book, Walmgate had degenerated drastically, pubs and inns supposedly outnumbered the houses, and those domestic dwellings were occupied by poverty-stricken families living in filthy conditions, crammed into tiny hovels in the alleyways off the street that, in Mary's day, had been taken up by small gardens and open spaces.

Today, Walmgate presents an interesting jumble of buildings from different periods, with a plethora of letting agents, hairdressers, charity shops and tattooists. The oldest apparent extant features recognisable to Mary would be the fourteenth-century timber-framed Bowes Morrell House, along with St Margaret's and St Deny's churches (the only two survivors of the six medieval churches once standing in Walmgate), and Mary must have been aware of the once dubious reputation of the unscrupulous tradesmen in neighbouring Fossgate (once aptly known as 'Tricksters Lane'), though thankfully the stench of fish on the prevailing breeze from Fossgate's one time fish market was no longer an issue.

In a street occupied by neighbouring traders, innkeepers, rag merchants, woollen warehouses and other retailers typical of the district and period, was Mary Tuke an exception then in acting as sole proprietress of her business? The concept of a 'business woman' in the eighteenth century may seem somewhat unconventional, however the seeds of women's independence had been sown (though shallow rooted as later history would attest) during the Commonwealth period succeeding the English Civil War in the previous century. Though opportunity was limited in the still deeply entrenched patriarchal society, women had gained a measure of autonomy in household management and business. At this time, women began to be trusted with significant traditional male roles thanks to a climate

Two somewhat dilapidated views of Walmgate, the left drawn by H. Cave in 1823 and, below, an engraving of a house in Walmgate contemporary to Mary Tuke's day. (*Both courtesy of The Evelyn Collection*)

St Deny's church, Walmgate.

where the emergence of new forms of worship, such as Quakerism, fostered a measure of latitude in a society where it was impossible to segregate entirely the spiritual and secular worlds.

Yet, in a later work by Sarah Stickney Ellis, Quaker turned Congregationalist and the author of numerous 'improving' books mostly written about women's role in society, her *Daughters of England* published in 1842 includes the admonition that 'if a lady does but touch any article, no matter how delicate, in the way of trade, she loses caste, and ceases to be a lady'. Whether or not Mary was flying in the face of domestic ideology, her enterprise lay at the heart of the family business.

Though Mary's decision might still be viewed as an unusual step for the time, possibly due to the common misconception that female entrepreneurship was a rarity in an age where female legal rights to own property, or control their own assets, was severely restricted (and in some spheres frowned upon as attested to by the strictures of Mrs Stickney Ellis), these legal restrictions only applied to married women. As Mary possessed the prodigious advantage of spinsterhood, as such she was actually relatively free to operate and achieve economic independence. In fact, it may have been her single state that was the driving force behind the establishment of the grocery business in Walmgate, one of simple economic necessity in supporting the family, never mind whether or not her own or her family's 'respectability' might be undermined, though she was obviously possessed of some social standing among her peers, Mary variously described as coming from one of York's 'prominent Quaker families'.

Regardless of whether Mary Tuke began her grocery business in Walmgate out of necessity or independent choice, we can only hypothesis as to why Mary had not married. In spite of the Quaker belief in equal worth, this did not protect women against the hazards and sorrows precipitated by married life – namely that of childbirth. In the eighteenth century, parents could have no confidence that their children could be born safely and thrive. The infant mortality rate (that is for a baby dying under one year of age) was a shocking 50 per cent. Childbirth itself was a dangerous process. Any complication could have a fatal outcome, sepsis and puerperal fever taking many mother's lives. Mary's father, William Tuke, lost his first wife Sarah Merry on 12 March 1692, less than a month after the death of their infant on 17 February; their first child Samuel had died in October 1690 aged just two days. William married his second wife, Mary's mother, Rebecka Smith, in 1693 and their first child, named for his father, was born on 25 October 1694 and died the following February. Of William and Rebecka's seven children, three were recorded as having died in infancy.

In an age where an estimated one in ten women could expect to die in childbirth or from related causes, on average a woman would become pregnant five or six times during her married life, and given that up to 10 per cent of the resultant labours proved fatal, this equated to a 41–47 per cent chance of dying during her reproductive life. Mary may then have had good reason to prefer to remain in the single state, or perhaps she simply chose to retain her independence.

While English Common Law dispossessed any woman who married, going so far as to forbid engagement in any financial transaction in her own right, an adult unmarried

Tuke family graves in the secluded Quaker burial ground, Bishophill.

Quaker Meeting *c.* 1809.

woman (whether spinster or widowed) was considered to have the legal status of *femme sole*, with the right to own property and make contracts in her own name. As such, in the eighteenth century, many single women operated freely in business, whether as sole traders, partners or freelance, some successfully evolving their business to head up their own thriving enterprises – from milk maids to milliners, seamstresses and slop sellers, even female smugglers and highway-women existed. However, in Mary's case there was another influential factor in favour of her commercial independence other than that of her marital status, and this lay in her Quakerism.

The Quaker movement (synonymous with the inception and shaping of the chocolate industry in York) was long-standing in the city. It was in York that George Fox, the founder of the Society of Friends, was thrown down the steps of the Minster in 1651 for preaching against the established church. Mary Tuke's full ancestral Quaker heritage and the influence of the Friends movement on the city will be examined in a later chapter, but suffice to say one of the cornerstones of Quakerism pertinent to Mary's situation was the movement's advocation of equality between the genders, preaching that *all* were children of God and members of a universal fellowship; a rather radical notion in the Georgian era, and beyond.

A Quaker women's independence within the family and community was fully accepted and in no way dependant on her marital condition – and in any case, deference to the husband was not deemed necessary, as a wife's self-reliance was attributed to the sharing equally of 'all the business of the society'. A contemporary outside observer of English Quakers in the early nineteenth century, Thomas Clarkson noted that the unmatched involvement of Quaker women in the affairs of the society,

> [G]ives them, in fact, a new cast of character. It produces in them, a considerable knowledge of human nature. It produces in them thought, and foresight, and judgment ... It elevates in them a sense of their own dignity and importance.

Also of importance to Mary, Quakers held a distinct advantage within the sphere of business, namely the confirmed reputation that they had built for themselves with regard to honesty and reliability in all things (paralleled by their quest for justice, equality and social reform). In an age where bartering was the norm, Quakers were among the first to set a firm price for goods and a fair one at that. Hence the customer knew where they stood with a Quaker business person, and appreciated Quaker retailers' ethical approach, which in turn gave them a commercially competitive edge over their rivals.

However, there was one stumbling block in the path to Mary building a thriving business, and that was the Merchant Adventurers' Company. To be able to trade in the city, merchants had to be both Freemen of the City of York and a member of the company. As a woman, Mary could only join the Merchant Adventurers' as the daughter or widow of an existing or former member. While Mary had managed to gain the status of Freeman by naming her father as a deceased member – the inscription on the Freeman's Roll of the City of York runs 'Maria Tuke, spinster Fil Willelmi Tuke, blacksmith', this was not enough alone to allow Mary to trade. She failed to fit the company membership criteria and consequently ended up trading without the necessary licence. In defiance of a subsequent court order and repeated summonses to court – though she was given six months to dispose of her shop goods – Mary continued to trade while battling the company's attempts to put her out of business. The imposition of fines and continued threats of imprisonment were the company's weapons in a prolonged battle against her that lasted nearly eight years. But Mary's tenacity won through, and after failing to force her business to capitulate, the Merchant Adventurers relented. Mary was allowed to continue to trade on payment of a token annual 10*s* fine, so long as she promised to buy all her goods locally. Then, in 1732, the company acquiesced further and Mary was granted permission to trade for the rest of her life after making a one-off payment of £10. Perhaps, after such a lengthy wrangle, the Merchant Adventurers Company ceded ground rather than imperil the preservation of their own dignity; at heart genuinely too altruistic to drive an enterprising woman out of business. Hypothesising sentiment aside, Mary made the one-off payment and Tukes continued to trade.

As well as stocking the specialities of tea, coffee and chocolate (sold in cakes that had to be boiled with milk or water), and other 'exotic' consumables such as sugar, spices, tobacco and snuff, imported foodstuffs came to play a central role in everyday life and consumption during the eighteenth century. Tukes Grocerys would have retailed all the usual grocery staples on offer – and in ranges priced for the discerning gentry's table to goods within the reach of poorer customers, from luxury to utility.

As to why Mary opted to enter the grocery trade, her choice of business would have been determined by the governing factor of her sex. The concentration of female business activity had been traditionally limited to a number of trades centring on three areas, namely those of clothing, food and drink, spheres of business arguably designated as 'female trades'. Typically, women were engaged in dressmaking, millinery and haberdashery, and as hosiers, linen drapers, grocers, chandlers, victuallers and coffee house keepers. Conversely, the male-dominated sectors included finance, manufacturing, agriculture and livestock management, architecture, building, furnishing and transport. This bolsters the view that women were effectively confined to entrepreneurial roles that equated to the economic servicing of a domestic nature, and in many instances, utilising their home as business premises too. It

Above: The Merchant Adventurers' Hall. This fourteenth-century guildhall was one of the most important buildings in the medieval city.

Right: 'Morning Chocolate'. Pietro Longhi's depiction of the luxury of chocolate consumption in the late 1770s.

Though well over a century after Mary Tuke had begun to trade, this reconstruction of a typical grocery shop interior *c.* 1860 shows the shelf and drawer set-up still evident. (*Courtesy of Beamish Museum*)

would not have been untypical for some early retailers to simply pile up goods for sale in a room, possibly in a space where the family also lived and slept. The plate glass for windows that would revolutionise shop displays would not become commonplace until the late nineteenh century, when the advent of manufacturing processes made such glazing more financially accessible. Enticement of customers then was reliant on perhaps a few oranges or a stick of black sugar (liquorice) displayed in the domestic window indicating that a grocery shop was kept therein.

We can only guess as to the look and layout of Tuke's Grocerys – but as the business prospered, we can assume that Mary would probably have invested in the appearance and functionality of her retail space – a step up from the piles of goods alluded to earlier, it became common for grocers to fit out their shops with a counter, shelves and drawers. Of course, the visual appeal of the goods would have been impaired, the introduction of gas lighting a long way off; a tallow candle sputtering on the counter would have sufficed. However, such interior fittings allowed for the separation and storage of products, as well as affording the opportunity of a display space, creative presentation of sugar loaves and boxes and baskets of items helping to sell goods that would have been far from eye-catching before the advent of branded packaging, appearing later in the nineteenth century.

Though chocolate, or cocoa, was initially beyond the economic reach of all but the very rich, along with tea and coffee, all three commodities had become more freely available by the time Mary set up shop in York (by the 1720s the preclusively high import duties on cocoa beans were no longer an issue), and with tobacco added to the list of popular stock, such commodities were not only profitable but a means of attracting fresh customers.

As the small grocery shop prospered, in 1746 Mary's teenaged nephew William Tuke joined her as an apprentice in the business, but by this time something else had drastically altered in Mary's life – she had married. Her nephew's Apprentice Indenture runs 'William Tuke, son of Samuel Tuke to Mary Frankland of York, grocer, 1746', confirming that Mary had married, though sadly by the date of the indenture she was already widowed.

We do not know exactly when Henry Frankland had taken her hand, but we do know that during their married life Mary had retained her independence and her grocery business. In fact, Henry abandoned his own profession, that of 'stuff weaver' (manufacturer of coarse cloth) to join Mary in the shop, and himself in turn had his own 'run-in' with the Merchant Adventurers Company. The company's court records for the session held on 1 July 1735 list one Henry Frankland among others as 'following the trade of grocer without having served an apprenticeship to that business'. However, the couple's financial circumstances were such that Henry was able to pay for his admission to the 'Freedom of the Fellowship', becoming a bona fide member of the company. Yet five years later, Henry was dead, leaving Mary a childless widow aged forty-four and sole proprietress of Tuke's Grocers once again.

When Mary herself died in 1752, having no children of her own, she left her twenty-year-old nephew William all her property. After some initial hesitation, William decided to continue with the family business, now located on the corner of Coppergate and Castlegate, having moved from Walmgate in Mary's lifetime. Now manufacturing chocolate as well as retailing it, producing the successful 'Tuke's Superior Rock Cocoa', the same year William came into his inheritance he became a Freeman Grocer and member of the monopolising Merchant Adventurers who had been so troubling to his aunt.

The business was to continue in family hands. In 1785, whether from a sense of familial duty or Quaker induced altruism, or perhaps both, William's son Henry abandoned the medical degree he was halfway through studying for to join his father. And it was this father and son partnership that took the business to new levels, with the introduction of 'Tukes' British Cocoa Coffee', 'Tuke's Rich Cocoa', 'Tukes' Plain Chocolate' and 'Tukes' Milk Chocolate' (not yet the solid bar you might buy in a shiny wrapper today but a chocolate used for mixing with milk to make a cocoa drink).

But the business wasn't everything to William; responsive to his Quaker ethics, he was responsible for establishing The Retreat in York, where the revolutionary humane treatment of the mentally ill paved the way for modern treatment of psychiatric disorders. This legacy and other philanthropic acts of the Tukes and the Rowntrees will be discussed later in 'A Question Of Belief'.

Henry Tuke (1755–1814) and his son, Samuel (1784–1857), as well as carrying on the reforming philanthropic ventures initiated by William, continued with the business that would remain in the Tuke family for several decades. Until in 1862, when Henry Isaac Rowntree bought out the cocoa division of Tuke & Co.

Henry Isaac's father Joseph Rowntree senior, with his own flourishing grocery business located in Pavement, was a fellow Quaker and good friend of Samuel Tuke's. In 1860, Henry Isaac had gone to work in the Tuke cocoa business in Castlegate, and soon after became manager of the cocoa, chocolate and chicory department. It was the legacy from Joseph senior's will that enabled Henry Isaac to purchase the Tuke Company; after the death of Samuel Tuke in 1857 as the family's interest in the business had waned. The change of business was announced thus:

Rowntree's Grocers can be seen to the right of this photograph. (*Courtesy of The Evelyn Collection*)

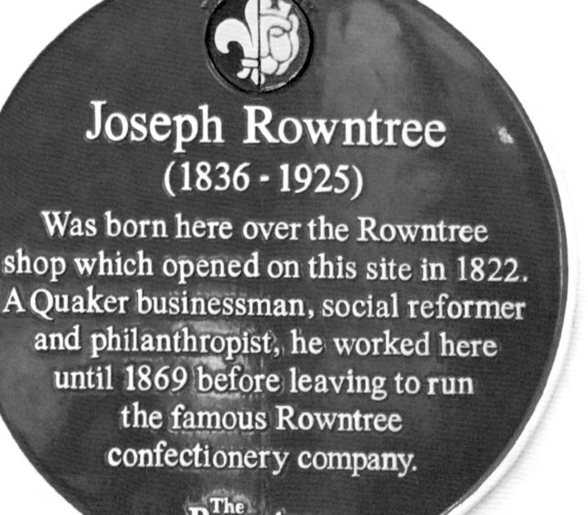

The premises at No. 28 Pavement where the Rowntree family grew up is now a Pizza Hut; at the time of writing this book the building was swathed with scaffolding, the upstairs undergoing renovation into flats.

> We have to inform you that we have relinquished the manufacture of Cocoa, Chocolate and Chicory in favour of our friend, H. I. Rowntree, who has been for some time practically engaged on the concern, and whose knowledge of the business in its several departments enables us with confidence to recommend him to the notice of our connection.
> We remain very respectfully,
> Tuke and Company,
> York. 1st of 7th month of 1862.

Though Tuke's Superior Rock Cocoa – the blend of pure cocoa and sugar compressed into a form of cake selling at ninepence a pound wholesale – was an esteemed product in York, the company ran at a loss during the first year that it was under Henry Isaac's management. In spite of the gloomy profit margin, the decision was taken to invest in a 'wonderful new machine' to grind cocoa, and to relocate the business to more expansive premises. By 1864, the firm had moved to the four-storey block facing the south-west end of Lendal Bridge, bounded by Tanner's Moat, Wellington Row and Queen Street. Though collectively comprising an ironworks, a tavern and several cottages in various states of dilapidation and disrepair, the site's proximity to the railway station and road and river transport links made this an ideal location.

At this time, only the Dutch firm Van Houten possessed the exclusive secret of a press that could extract much of the extraneous fat or cocoa butter from the bean, producing a purer cocoa essence or powder, which made a far more appetising hot drink, leaving the butter to be used in the production of eating chocolate. Consequently, in England in the 1860s, sales of eating chocolate were very small compared with the established drinking cocoa brands such as Rock, and two thirds of Rowntree's output from the Tanner's Moat factory were dedicated to rock cocoa. Steam-powered manufacturing processes were primitive and rudimentary, with a donkey cart delivering raw materials that had to be carried by hand up and down the building between each stage of manufacture. Active at shop floor level, it was not unusual to see Henry Isaac with rolled up sleeves and greasy hands.

The rebranding of 'Rowntree's Prize Medal Rock Cocoa', after the product was awarded a prize at the Yorkshire Fine Art and Industrial Exhibition of 1866, doubtless increased sales and enhanced the Rowntree reputation. And in 1869, elder brother Joseph, who was far more adept at concentrating on the accounts, joined the company, leaving Henry Isaac to deal with the manufacturing side of the business.

In 1881, Rowntree expanded their repertoire with the addition of gums and pastilles, a hitherto French speciality, leading to a great increase in the company's prosperity and a subsequent expansion in premises with the purchase of an old flour mill on North Street, adjoining Tanner's Moat.

After Henry Isaac's death in 1883 (he died of peritonitis aged forty-five), Joseph Rowntree continued solely to successfully develop the firm, so successfully in fact, that in 1906, Rowntree production moved entirely from the Tanner's Moat site to a state-of-the-art factory built on Haxby Road in the north of the city. Joseph Rowntree had purchased 29 acres of land in 1890 with the purpose-built factory in mind, conveniently close to a works branch of the North Eastern Railway that could deliver raw materials. From a workforce numbering a dozen men when Henry Isaac first acquired the Tuke's business, by 1862 employee numbers had increased to 100 by 1880, and by the time the Haxby Road site was in full production, Rowntree was employer to over 4,000 men and women in York.

Rowntree's Haxby Road site, seen from the air. (*Courtesy of The Evelyn Collection*)

Joseph Rowntree in 1862.

Could Mary Tuke ever have imagined, from her humble retail beginnings, her sole management spanning twenty-one years during which the reign of the first George had given way to that of the second Hanoverian sovereign, that the establishment of her shop would evolve into one of the great names in chocolate history? The commercial successes of which would be closely bound up with those other confectionery giants of York – Terry's and Craven's, whose inception, growth and development were formative in shaping modern York as a city of confectionery manufacture – 'Chocolate City', a city with a broader history in this industry than any other in the UK.

3

Standards of Living: Fair & Foul

By the time the railway revolution had seized York (the glorious age of steam began there when the first train chuffed its way out of a makeshift wooden station on Queen Street outside the walls of the city in 1839), cocoa manufacture was the second greatest employer in York, second only to the railways.

Latterly, the blend of corporate and social responsibility and the utilisation of females in a mixed workforce exercised by York's confectioners, in view of the industry's size, was to prove beneficially impactful on the employment dynamic in York, the extent of which had not been seen elsewhere in the UK.

However, as explored in Chapter One, York was a city in the grip of an economic decline at the beginning of the Georgian era; even the population levels had stagnated, and the vision of a York as a city of confectionery manufacturering giants was distant, if not unimaginable.

As we have seen, the restrictive and monopolising attitude of the Merchant Adventurers Company was certainly a major contributory factor to that decline. This trading association formed in 1357 still seemed to have its business ethics firmly planted in the medieval period. The company's insistence on the strict adherence to their regulations concerning the exclusivity of allowing only Freemen of the City to trade in York undeniably served to hinder economic growth, a short-sighted and archaic policy harking back to the halcyon days when York was once described as 'the foremost industrial town in the North of England.' Sadly no more. At a time when other northern towns were being swept up in what became known as the Industrial Revolution, York remained an industrial backwater. The prospect of the development of any heavy industry was precluded by the prohibitively high price of coal, which had to be shipped in from the coal fields of the East Riding, and with the expansion of existing commercial activity further compounded by the company's myopic attitude and woeful lack of foresight and enterprise, it comes as no surprise that economic progress and development were hobbled. In the shadow of its mightier metropolitan neighbours, York fulfilled the role of something of a parochial market town, servicing its own basic needs and those of the surrounding district.

Some small artisan industries did exist in York during the period under our scrutiny. There was leather-making in the tanneries located in Walmgate utilising the River Foss, and at Marygate on the Ouse, York was also an acknowledged centre for combmakers and

The railway station, York, 1861. (*Courtesy of The Evelyn Collection*)

John Varley's eighteenth-century view of York.

horn breakers, active around the area of the aptly named Hornpot Lane, off Petergate. But as Drake remarked in 1736,

> except some few wine merchants, the export of butter, and some small trifles not worth mentioning, there is no other trade carried on in the city of York at this day ... What has been, and is, the chief support of the city, at present, is the resort to and residence of several country gentlemen with their families in it.

In the extract above, he alludes to the burgeoning market that would alter York's fortunes for the better...

By the 1730s, the city was indeed well established as the social capital of the North, stimulating an economy that was responsive to the needs of the elite clientele now favouring the city. The advent of the turnpike had made it easier, and faster, to get to York from London, and other major towns around the UK. Termed as 'turnpike mania', the years

YORK Four Days
Stage-Coach.

Begins on Friday *the* 12*th.* of April. 1706.

ALL that are desirous to pass from *London* to *York*, or from *York* to *London*, or any other Place on that Road, Let them Repair to the *Black Swan* in *Holbourn* in *London*, and to the *Black Swan* in *Coney street* in *York*.

At both which Places, they may be received in a Stage Coach every *Monday*, *Wednesday* and *Friday*, which performs the whole Journey in Four Days, (*if God permits.*) And sets forth at Five in the Morning.

And returns from *York* to *Stamford* in two days, and from *Stamford* by *Huntington* to *London* in two days more. And the like Stages on their return.

Allowing each Passenger 14l. weight, and all above 3d. a Pound.

Performed By *Benjamin Kingman*, *Henry Harrison*, *Walter Baynes*,

Also this gives Notice that Newcastle Stage Coach, sets out from York, every Monday, and Friday, and from Newcastle every Monday, and Friday.

Recd. in pt 05.00.0 of Mr. Bodingfeld for 5 places for Monday the 3 of June 1706.

York Stage Coach timetable, dated 12 April 1706.

1751–72 saw an explosion in the expansion of toll roads, the driving principle behind which was that travellers contributing toward road repair maintained improved carriageways, where formerly principal highways for most of the year were reduced to dangerous, rutted and muddy tracks.

With the added attractions and delights of the Assembly Rooms, horse racing, the theatre and other social amenities, the attraction of local gentry and nobility from their seats in the county was a natural progression. The Prince of Wales, the future George IV, and his set of fashionable hangers-on came to York for the racing season, and in turn distinguished county families with illustrious names gravitated to the city – Fairfax, Scrope, Bourchier, Carr and Fitzwilliam – all drawn to York, and in their privileged wake other 'smart' friends from out of town.

The opportunities then for successfully establishing a host of service and catering industries had never been better, and in this climate, trade in eighteenth-century York was conducted by a greater variety of men and women than it had ever been before. Finally, with the dissipation of the Merchant Adventurers' influence and importance by this time, specific, specialised and luxury trades began to thrive, all providing the goods and services required by the fashionable frequenting the newly polite and elegant city fast becoming the playground of the wealthy.

And of course chocolate was among this litany of desirable, luxury consumables. The coffee and chocolate houses flourished (coffee houses were not exclusive to their name and also served chocolate to their customers), there were at least thirty such houses open in York in the eighteenth century, and those known by name, so there may have been many more. For the most part they were ephemeral and no one enterprise seems to have lasted out the whole century, but Harrison's, first in Petergate and later on Nessgate Corner, Iveson's, also in Petergate, and Duke's, near Ouse Bridge, all stayed the course for around fifty years.

The growth in the number of businesses then catering to the leisured classes, the now familiar and welcome sector characteristic of the new economic trend, engendered a climate that positively drove such enterprises and consequently trade, and, most importantly where standards of living were concerned, employment.

Of course, for those fortunate enough to have been born into the 'middling sort' or even further up the social scale, employment, livelihood and means would not have been their primary concern. In a position to enjoy their leisure, the day began by partaking of a light breakfast, often featuring a 'dish' of chocolate (the first English-made cups were sans handles in the traditional and fashionable Chinese style; not until the mid-1750s would handles be added to prevent the ladies from burning their fingers), chocolate that may well have been purchased from a grocers like Tukes on the instruction of the mistress of the house.

Domestic direction as to where to purchase the best of such comestibles, along with other household concerns were a matter of daily discussion between mistress and housekeeper, along with matters such as the behaviour of the servants or what would be served for dinner that evening. In their smart residences, such as those in Bootham and Micklegate that reflected the importance and prosperity of their Georgian occupants, people would engage in the genteel tasks of letter writing or practicing the piano.

Ladies might receive calls or visit others, while for the gentlemen a visit to Mr Atkinson, 'linen draper, silk mercer and men's mercer' at No. 12 Little Stonegate might beckon, or to Todd's bookshop, a short stroll away at The Sign of the Bible. Wolstenholme's also sold books at the corner of Petergate and Minster Gates, and for those wishing to increase their fortunes, in common with most booksellers, Wolstenholme's also sold lottery tickets,

A wealthy lady is served chocolate at breakfast in Jean-Étienne Liotard's *The First Breakfast*, painted in 1754.

The genteel Georgian occupation of letter writing.

View of the houses and shop at east end of York Minster, W. Richardson. (*Courtesy of The Evelyn Collection*)

another channel for the obsessive gambling that was a national and classless phenomenon, which will be examined later.

Weather permitting, perhaps a promenade along the New Walk, to see and be seen, before returning to the heart of the city for an afternoon spent in one or other of the numerous coffee or chocolate houses, catching up on current affairs either by perusing the newspapers assiduously provided by the management, or listening to or participating in the general discussion so prevalent in the atmosphere of what had come to be known as 'coffee house society'.

However, while York was experiencing an upturn in its declining fortunes, the chocolate industry that was having such an impact on the city's later industrial prosperity was still in its infancy, and with no large-scale manufacturers established to provide badly needed employment, in the words of the Biblical Matthew, 'The poor will always be with us.' An examination of this needy diametric of York's population is warranted in view of the philanthropic measures that prominent members of the city's chocolate elite would later become involved with.

York, the same as any other metropolis in this period, was a city burdened with a very large number of poor inhabitants, and decades would pass before the altruistic actions of Joseph Rowntree were to reach fruition and make any sizeable social impact on the situation. Much of the population lived in poverty, and additionally there were in the region of 500 paupers

A poor and prolific family in a slum area of York. (*Courtesy of York Museums Trust*)

recorded each year in the 1720s, those individuals not merely 'hard up' but in such dire straits they were eligible for poor relief.

In common with other towns and cities, York had developed a 'slum quarter' centered around the Water Lanes district, three streets that led from the River Ouse to Castlegate. In the nineteenth century they were known as the First Lane, Middle Lane and Far Water Lane, and had long held a sour reputation for their unsanitary living conditions and high levels of crime bred in squalid surroundings. Much of York's cholera problems not surprisingly started in these streets; the improvement commissioners in the 1840s discovered an appalling standard of living had long been prevalent, and the toilet facilities for the residents were nearly non-existent. They noted 'the inhabitants have to use those of their neighbours by stealth or go into the street', a situation that had existed since habitation of the area began in the twelfth century.

During the period that is the focus of this book, the average 'poor' family would together have occupied one room. Though scantily furnished, the space would have been inevitably cramped in the absence of any effective birth control. Inhabitants paid a weekly rent in the region of 2*s*, possibly less for a room in a cellar or under some creaky eaves, to give an idea of relative costs of living, during the eighteenth century wages could be as low as £2 to £3 per year for a domestic servant. Of course female domestic servants earned less than men, and as ever manual labour could be bought even more cheaply, for example a porter could expect a penny for shifting a bushel of coal, while for chopping wood the going rate was 1½*d* per hour. A beggar could expect a farthing in alms, twopence if he were lucky.

Conversely, the middling sort could expect to live comfortably for an annual expenditure of £100, while the gulf between the 'middling sort' and the simply rich was

Right: First Waters Lane. (*Courtesy of The Evelyn Collection*)

Below: York Castle Museum's reconstruction of the typical domestic space that a poor family would have been economically forced to occupy. (*Courtesy of York Museums Trust*)

in the region of £500 a year. A great divide then between the top and bottom rungs of the class ladder, where the sixpence charged by a barber to dress a gentleman's wig would secure a 4 pound loaf of bread, hopefully unadulterated by an unscrupulous baker to bring up the weight.

If the poor occupants of such a single room were lucky, they would be living in the vicinity of a shared standpipe, which would have delivered water at intervals, for the waterworks supplied only part of the city, and then only on certain days. Supply would be further rendered sporadic by the condition of the water 'trees' – piping in the form of hollowed out lengths of elm, themselves inefficient and requiring frequent repair at the joints; leakage from those on Ouse Bridge between 1710 and 1711 was thought to have damaged the structure of the bridge itself. The water supplied by these inadequate pipes was pumped, unfiltered, directly from the Ouse. The river itself was the recipient of the overflow liquid wastes from slaughterhouses, dung heaps and pigsties around the city, effluent that the archaic underground drains were ill capable of dealing with. These drains and sewers in turn also discharged into the Ouse, albeit at a lower point downriver. However, this was still upstream to where the Ouse Waterworks obtained their supply! The second and equally important source of water was drawn from wells around the city, though these were seldom less contaminated than the filthy waters from the river, as in places the aquifer from which the springs issued were said to be buried beneath several feet of 'the rubbish of centuries', if not otherwise tainted by the run-off from burial grounds.

Those who could afford it and who were living in 'houses of the higher classes and all the more respectable houses recently built' would privately filter their water supply, the Rowntrees were known to have filtered the water drawn from their well in Blossom Street. Though such measures were of scant effectiveness in the face of waterborne pathogens, it was a luxury that many, predominantly the poor, had to do without, most of them taking water directly from the rivers like the Foss, which, having been dammed at Castle Mills, was 'a stagnant water replete with vegetable and animal matters'.

Concerning that other domestic necessity alluded to and virtually non-existent in the Waters Lane district of the city, again those of means could enjoy the convenience (excuse the pun) of water closets emptying directly into drains or cess pits (which probably flowed into the Ouse.) However, the more down to earth shared one privy, with upwards of fourteen other families. Privy contents were taken by cart and shovelled onto one of the city's dunghills; one such large heap habitually festered close to Layerthorpe Bridge, and a number of smaller piles in the vicinity of the Foss must have supplemented the already fetid waters. (It was on to one of the city's public dung hills that the body of Catholic martyr Margaret Clitheroe was unceremoniously slung post execution by 'pressing' on Ouse Bridge. Some six weeks later, however, her body was exhumed by a group of dedicated Catholics who gave Margaret a Christian burial, minus her hand, which remains preserved as a holy relic at the Bar Convent in York to this day.)

By the late eighteenth century, the City Corporation was making some effort to curtail pollution of the Ouse at the Staithe by forbidding any delay in the loading of dung onto soil-carrying vessels, along with the removal of a 'necessary house' (forerunner of the public lavatory) and a communal 'soil hole' also located there. Despite these salutary measures, the city's drains continued to empty their contents into the rivers throughout the century.

Especially for the poor then, staying alive must have been challenging to say the least. With no organised refuse collections other than a sole 'scavenger' employed by the Corporation, who cleared only those pavements and streets directly in front of Corporation premises (this responsibility would eventually extend to all streets and pavements within the city, but not

Ouse Bridge painted by Thomas Girtin in 1800. (*Courtesy* Yale Center for British Art, Paul Mellon Collection)

until 1786), and compounded by indifferent drainage, the filthy water supply and woeful provision for public health, it comes as no surprise that the average adult life expectancy was 36.6 years; for those inhabiting a crowded and disease-ridden environment this would inevitably have been reduced, perhaps even to the mid-twenties.

Of course, in a city such as York, as in any other at this time, sporadic outbreaks of disease were commonplace. However, between the summers of 1718 and 1719 the typhus epidemic that swept through the city was particularly virulent, the death toll peaking during the warmer months and exacerbated by the unusually hot summer of 1719, the epidemic taking a real hold at the beginning of May that year, and reaching its height in July and lasting all of August. Mortality rates remained high into the years 1721–23 due to the outbreak of a smallpox epidemic, followed later in the decade by a serious outbreak of probable influenza in the early winter of 1729. As well as waterborne typhus, 'King Cholera' also stalked York's street, with the epidemic of 1832 claiming its first victim, one Thomas Hughes, a twenty-one-year-old waterman who lived in a filthy yard at Skeldergate, and fell ill on 3 June. The death toll would reach 185 for this particular outbreak, fifty-six of the victims living in Skeldergate alone. The Medical Board of York took what preventative measures they could. At their first meeting, provision for the burial of cholera victims was discussed, as well as the difficulties and relative risks of transporting the dead through the city (one angry incident had already erupted resulting in the coffin of a cholera victim being knocked from the cart and breaking open in the street). As to where the dead should be buried, the law required that cholera burials be at least one foot below ground level, therefore burial in any of York's already full graveyards was out of the question. The board were aware of some available wasteland owned by York Corporation that could be utilised, near the

One of York's surviving cholera burial grounds, near to the railway station.

dog-kennel, not far from Thief Lane, and further burial grounds were dotted around the city, one of which can still be seen today, a small grassed area close to York station.

It was in fact a native of York, John Snow, born in the poor and frequently flooded district centring on North Street in low proximity to the west bank of the Ouse, who is considered one of the fathers of modern epidemiology, in part because of his work in tracing the source of the cholera outbreak of 1854 to a public water pump in London's Soho.

With regards to feeding probably several hungry mouths (the average size of a 'poor' family at this time was seven – if they hadn't been killed off by the filthy drinking water) the practicalities of cooking a family meal in the cramped conditions of single-roomed lodgings were severely restrictive. The local baker's oven could often be utilised for a small fee if he were not baking bread at the time, but not everyone could afford meat or perhaps even pastry for a pie, in which case bread could be purchased from a corner shop, though it might be heavily adulterated with alum or chalk to make it look white, and as likely to cause intestinal distress as chalk-thickened milk, vinegar diluted with sulphuric acid or confectionery and pickles coloured with copper salts. Other foodstuff within the pecuniary reach of the poor might include small bunches of stale greens, a farthing's worth of cheese or paper twists of tea-flavoured dust, alternatively, for those hungry enough to swallow their pride, scraps could be begged from rich men's houses. Of course, this doesn't take into account consumption of alcohol; a 'labouring man' could be expected to consume upwards of six pints of beer a day – calorifically equivalent to an uneatable quantity of bread, beer was essential in maintaining the physical stamina of manual workers. Here then enter the Quakers and their promotion of chocolate.Marketed as 'more than a drink a food', they worked to challenge this reliance on beer, as substitute chocolate provided sustenance as well as refreshment – Quaker cocoa was a temperance drink.

As well as The Friends' embrasure of chocolate as a healthy alternative to alcohol, Quakers also strove to alleviate social inadequacy. In York, William Tuke was instrumental in the establishment of The Retreat, an innovative establishment at the time advocating humane treatment for the mentally ill, as well as helping to found and develop the educational establishments of the Ackworth School in 1779. In 1818, he put forward the first proposal for the educational establishment that would become Bootham School, and assisted with the founding of the Trinity Lane Quaker Girls' School, a precursor of the Mount School.

Joseph Rowntree Senior also took significant steps to ease and assist those of the city's population in need, York's population having virtually doubled between 1821 and 1861 (augmented in the 1840s with the influx of Irish immigrants whose homeland had been decimated by famine and political unrest).

In 1831, Rowntree Senior became a member of the Improvement Commission, endeavouring to address the problems of insanitary housing, a direct product of the ineffective sewrage disposal discussed earlier, the River Foss at that time still effectively an overblown gutter emptying directly into the Ouse, and rendering Foss Island a swamp. His concerns were not limited to the counteraction of repeated epidemics, however. In 1846, he was the chief proponent in setting up an annual winter soup kitchen for the cold and hungry. Further troubled by the inadequate educational provision for the poor (in 1826 a doorstep survey of the labouring poor highlighted that a quarter of the six to ten year olds did not attend any school, and a significant number in the twelve to fourteen year age group could neither read nor write), by 1828 Rowntree was one of those involved in the setting up of the Hope Street British School, and later in 1848 was to pioneer a First-Day (or Sabbath) school for boys aged eight to sixteen, later developing into an adult school from which the York Adult School movement developed.

Dublin slum dwellers. Many Irish immigrants swelled York's poor population in the 1840s.

Following in his father's footsteps, Joseph Rowntree Junior adopted a unique approach to poverty, at a time when there was little sympathy or understanding of what poverty even meant. Significantly, Joseph Rowntree understood the importance of drawing attention to the need to tackle the root causes of poverty, and not just its immediate consequences. Later generations would benefit from Joseph Rowntree's attempts to improve the quality of his employees' lives, introducing professional standards for his workforce, the provision of a free library and free education for workers aged under seventeen. A social welfare officer, doctor and a dentist were also employed to provide free services and look after the wellbeing of the Rowntree workforce. Joseph Rowntree also donated £10,000 in 1906 to establish a pension fund for his workers. On a more day-to-day fundamental level, one of his main innovations was to give workers a say in the appointment of their immediate supervisors.

While the Rowntree philanthropic approach, and those of other notable Quakers paving the way for social reform, will be examined in more detail in 'A Question of Belief', recognition must be given to the inter-playing dynamics that brought about the subsequent improvements in social standards as a direct result of the formation of the chocolate industry as the foremost economic drive for York. While the Quakers appear in the vanguard of these improving efforts, the two other major confectionery producers who were integral to the birth of 'Chocolate City' also played their part and are deserving of recognition too, not only in their concerns for the plight of those less fortunate than themselves, but in the eventual generation of gender equitable employment opportunities, and the betterment of consumer standards.

Both Joseph Terry and Mary Craven produced confectionery on the strict basis that only the best was good enough. This principle of commercial integrity was in line with the Tuke and Rowntree firm Quaker ethic that as a matter of conscience no foodstuff should ever be adulterated. In an era where it was common practice to 'stretch' raw ingredients with often poisonous additions, in 1836 Joseph Terry assisted with the formation of an association in London, to protect the consumer against adulterations to confectioners' and lozenge makers' products.

As well as the obvious financial advantages garnered, the development of York as 'Chocolate City' then had a direct influence on the wellbeing of the city's populace. The circumstances and determining factors of the industry's beginnings breeding an economic environment where those forging successful commercial endeavours could in turn lay the foundations for later improvement, through welfare and employment opportunity.

York today is recognised as having the strongest and most flourishing economy in the north of England, and while over a number of years the city has reinvented itself from a centre of confectionery manufacturing into an international hub for science and technology, as well as a national centre for financial and business services, as home to a diverse and dynamic range of businesses, employment in the confectionery industry and commercial off-shoots, as we shall see later, still remain significant.

4

Leisure & Pleasure in Georgian York

In its confirmed position as the social capital of the North, naturally the York of the Georgian era was esteemed as a destination for the 'polite and elegant', although this was also an age of strident social contrasts, where exuberant decadence existed alongside shameful poverty. There were, however, pastimes and pleasures for every echelon of society to enjoy; an impromptu jig struck up at a May fair to the tune of a fiddle mirrored at the very lowest level the sophisticated evenings of dancing held beneath the glittering chandeliers of the York Assembly Rooms; hundreds of guineas won and lost at the faro or basset table equitable with the few shillings lost in a game of crooked dice in one of York's many taverns.

From the savage to the sedate, bear-baiting to shopping for brocades, the Georgian inhabitants of York enjoyed all the delights the city had to offer. For the monied clientele, to whom the city catered so well, the diversions were legion. Epitomising the striven for elegance of the era, the assembly rooms, or the Burlington Rooms as they were so named for their illustrious designer, perhaps presented the best platform for the display of opulence that had become the mainstay of York's rising status as the northern playground for the fashionable and rich. Noted as Yorkshire's finest example of Palladian architecture, work on building Lord Burlington's fashionable destination was begun in 1730 on the current site the rooms occupy in Blake Street, and in stark contrast to the small timbered dwellings then lining the neighbouring streets.

The assembly rooms were first used during Race Week in August 1732 (what we know today as Ebor Week and still an enormous draw to the city). Gatherings often proved something of a marriage market, where a useful introduction might be made, or the eye of an eligible beau might alight upon a young lady, kept at arms' length while dancing the quadrille or cotillion, though country dances were the more popular tread, affording greater opportunity for hand-holding.

After all, in the words of Jane Austen's Charlotte Lucas in *Pride & Prejudice*, marriage 'was the only honourable provision for well-educated young women of small fortune.' In order then to protect satin slippers from the dirt and filth of the streets a 'chair' was a must. Conveyance in a sedan chair would have cost sixpence for half a mile before ten in the evening, after ten o'clock the cost rose to a shilling, provided you didn't order the chairmen to stop for too long, perhaps to gossip with a friend (the 'meter' froze so to speak, unless the halt exceeded ten minutes). After depositing their passenger in the grand portico of the assembly rooms, chairmen would wait out the assembly for the homeward fares in the basement, where their recent earnings were often staked at dice and cards. There was plenty

The assembly rooms. (*Courtesy of The Evelyn Collection*)

Five Positions of Dancing. The illustrations of dancers show foot positions for a beginner, while the line drawings below each dancer show the positions of a 'finish'd Dancer'.

of gambling going on above stairs too – those not disposed dance preferred instead to play for high stakes at hazard or piquet in the 'Round Room'. It would seem that gambling, in virtually any form, was a Georgian obsession; and though it seemed most endemic and excessive in the upper classes, wagering was in no way exclusive to this set, the lower classes as adept at losing money as their social superiors.

As well as roulette, popular card games of the time included faro, piquet, whist, vingt et un (better known today as 'twenty-one' or 'blackjack'), and the higher class baccarat and hazard, the latter played with dice, not cards, for massive stakes, with the loss of an entire family estate not unknown at this time.

Other wagers could prove equally ruinous however. In 1756, *The Gentleman's Magazine* reported a £500 wager between Lord Rockingham and Lord Orford betting on the outcome of five turkeys and five geese raced between Norwich market and the Mile End turnpike! Equally bizarre was the bet placed by two members of White's (the London gentlemen's club famous for its betting book facilitating wagers on literally anything), who placed odds on the number of cats that would walk down opposite sides of the street, and it was members of Brooks', another gentlemen's club, who callously wagered on the life of a man who apparently fell down dead on the street outside – the suggestion that someone should go and see if he could be revived regarded as very poor taste since it might affect the outcome of the bet.

Of course, horse racing presented ample opportunity to gamble, and York, known as the Ascot of the North, has a tradition of horse racing that can be traced back into antiquity to the time when the Romans occupied the city. In the diary of Simon Scrope (descendant of the once eminent Scropes of Wensleydale who later bred Danby Cade, a famous race horse in the eighteenth century) the entry for 31 July 1730 runs:

> Every year there be more noble lords, gentle dames, and commoners of high and low degree at York for the races ... all of one mind, looking on York as the place above all others for sport and sportsmen...

Gambling at an early roulette table, *c.* 1800.

While race meets had been held in various suitable open spaces around the city, on Acomb Moor, in the Forest of Galtres, where a famous annual race for a golden bell was run, and even on the frozen over River Ouse between Micklegate Tower and Skeldergate Postern, by the early eighteenth century, Clifton was the established venue. However, the frequently boggy conditions precipitated by the flooding Ouse was the overriding factor in the City Corporation's decision to find an alternative site for a new and improved race course. The year after Simon Scrope's diary entry, in 1731, York Races relocated to the Knavesmire, where races are still run today. It was astutely timed to follow on from the summer assizes in August (today the Ebor handicap is still run in August), when the city's capacity was swelled with landed gentry who had travelled in from the surrounding countryside for court business. As racing became ever more organised and popular, attending York Races became something of a social scene, attracting crowds exceeding 100,000 spectators. Spectator numbers were further supplemented by those come to witness the public executions carried out on the York Tyburn, or the 'three-legged mare' as it was known, and conveniently sited opposite the new racecourse, adding to the entertainment, some racegoers even placed tasteless bets on how long it would take a convicted criminal to die on the gallows, alongside a wager on runners and riders.

The great popularity of York Races also increased the desire of those in 'polite society' to distance themselves from the hoi polloi of the lower class crowds, who enjoyed the additional attractions of the ever-present sideshows, fortune tellers and wandering musicians. Consequently, in 1754, at the instigation of the Marquess of Rockingham, the first grandstand was built at a cost of £1,250 by the architect John Carr. Overlooking the winning post, Carr's classically designed stand was opened on 25 August 1755, allowing for additional 'elegant' viewing from the roof, weather permitting of course.

View of the grandstand on Knavesmire Racecourse, 1760. (*Courtesy of The Evelyn Collection*)

Out of the race season, there were still plenty of pleasures and diversions for rich and poor alike. The aspiring 'middling sort' could promenade on the New Walk, a tree-lined avenue created in the 1730s, which followed the River Ouse from Tower Gardens downstream for approximately 1 mile. The creation of one of England's first riverside walks was another of the City Corporation's bids to promote York in the eyes of *le bon ton*, a term commonly used to refer to Britain's high society during the Georgian era, implying good manners 'in the fashionable mode'. In raising and affirming York's status as that of a leading northern social centre for smart society, for the peerage, aristocracy and the emerging wealthy merchant and banking classes now merging with the ranks of higher society, while the landed families of ancient pedigree may have looked down their noses at those of the nouveau riche, their coin was equally as welcome to the city's economy as that of 'old money'. Thus the creation of the New Walk, initially stretching from Skeldergate Bridge to the junction where the River Foss joins the Ouse, afforded a unique opportunity for the fashionable to stroll alongside the riverbank, shaded by parallel rows of elm trees. The walk proved so popular that it was soon extended further out of the city, and to allow for the continuation of the New Walk, the original Blue Bridge was built in 1738. In keeping with the preference of the time for order and formality, hedges were planted to separate the gentrified promenade from the surrounding natural and wilder landscape, and perhaps the natural and wilder inhabitants of the city, those who might enjoy the baser distractions of the bear-garden or cock pit.

It would not be until 1835 that 'baiting' was prohibited by Parliament with the introduction of the Cruelty to Animals Act, and the savage entertainment of pitting specialised

The New Walk. (*Courtesy of The Evelyn Collection*)

breeds of dog such as mastiffs or old English bulldogs, specifically bred for baiting bulls, officially came to an end. Earlier attempts to curtail this cruel sport in England had been made by the Puritans; although when a number of spectators died after a stand collapsed in London's famous Bear Pit in Paris Gardens, the Puritans viewed this as a sign of God's displeasure in violating the Sabbath, as the calamity occurred on a Sunday afternoon, rather than as an act of retribution in the face of such cruelty in the name of sport.

Another exceedingly popular blood sport was cock fighting, said to be the world's oldest spectator sport, recorded 6,000 years ago in Persia. In York, the primary venue for the enjoyment of this barbaric amusement was in the grounds of Cock Pit House (now occupied by St Mary's House at No. 66 Bootham), where a cock pit was located adjacent to a bowling green, enjoyed by those with with more delicate sporting sensibilities.

It was possibly on the Cock Pit House bowling green (the large bowling green at Kings Manor was no longer in use by this time) that celebrated gentleman highwayman 'Swift Nick' Nevison secured his alibi against arrest for a murder he had committed in Kent that morning, making the celebrated ride to York (so often mistakenly attributed to Dick Turpin), arriving at sunset in time to make a wager with the Lord Mayor on the outcome of his game. Though later arrested for his crime, the mayor's unquestionable evidence secured Nevison's equital. In fact, it was cock fighting that indirectly led to the arrest and subsequent execution of infamous highwayman Dick Turpin at York's Tyburn; having shot his landlord's prize gamecock after an argument, Turpin then threatened to shoot the landlord as well as an agahst onlooker.

And as the gallows appearance of Turpin attests, public execution also proved a popular form of entertainment. On 7 April 1739, Dick Turpin was conveyed through the streets

Cock fight, 1808. (*Thomas Rowlandson*)

Rowlandson's 'Execution Day at York'.

of York in an open cart, bowing to the crowds that lined the route to the gallows, along Castlegate, over the Ouse Bridge and on along Ousegate, continuing up the slope to Micklegate. Driven underneath Micklegate Bar and onto Blossom Street, past The Mount and finally reaching the Knavesmire, Turpin faced his ultimate date with the noose.

After climbing the ladder to the gallows with a firm step (although he had to stamp down his right leg to stop it trembling) Turpin then spent half an hour chatting to the executioner and guards. Turpin's bravado did not fail him, as reported in the *York Courant,* as he 'with undaunted courage looked about him, and after speaking a few words to the topsman, he threw himself off the ladder and expired in about five minutes'. Turpin's real name was John Palmer, and in spite of being buried in a very deep grave in the churchyard of St Georges, Palmer/Turpin's body was later found disinterred and in the garden of one of the city surgeons. The illegal trade in cadavers for human dissection was big business at this time, so to prevent any further 'body snatching' attempts, the corpse of the rogue celebrity was reburied in St George's churchyard, this time however the coffin was filled with unslaked quicklime. His headstone can still be seen today.

Although the public nature of such spectacles was supposed to act as a deterrent to the populace, public hangings often took on a mass entertainment quality, perhaps akin to an open-air concert atmosphere today. Crowds including families with young children would bring along a picnic and make a day of it, and as mentioned previously, the York Tyburn's proximity to the racecourse made for double the entertainment value on a race day. Despite the obvious taste and enthusiasm for the spectacle of public execution, the ultimate decision to move the proceedings to York Castle Gaol was probably heavily influenced by the

John Palmer/Dick Turpin's grave in St George's churchyard, not far from Walmgate Bar.

objectionable initial impression of the city given by the Knavesmire gallows, located as they were next to one of the main highways into York. The gallows were also a cause of major road congestion, a parallel perhaps to the traffic jams resulting from the ghoulish curiosity or 'rubber necking' at the site of an accident today. In an article printed on 25 July 1800, the *York Herald* explained,

> Thus will be removed from one of the principal roads leading to the city that disagreeable nuisance, the gallows; and thus will the inhabitants and passengers be no longer interrupted, and their humanity hurt, by the leading of unfortunate people to the place of execution.

In consequence, in order that the 'entrance to the town should no longer be annoyed by dragging criminals through the streets' at a civic meeting it was decided that investment in a new gallows should be made, to wit the cost of that totalled £10 15*s*.

Though sensibility had won the day, the Knavesmire gallows or the 'old drop' as it was known, stood (albeit unused) for a further eleven years before finally being dismantled in 1812, a grim reminder of the ultimate judicial penalty.

Executions still formed the mainstay of free public entertainment for all classes, however. The 'New Drop', as it became known, was constructed by Joseph Halfpenny, joiner of Blake Street, York, and set up at the back of the castle in an area bounded by the Castle Mills Bridge and the River Ouse, roughly where the roundabout by St George's car park is today. Looking toward York Castle Museum, in the wall to the right is a small doorway through which the condemned prisoners were led. Completed by 8 March 1801, the first executions were not to take place until Saturday 28 August 1802, when James Roberts, William Barker and William Jackson were all hanged from the new gallows. The New Drop at the castle continued as York's principal place of execution, until the 1820s that is, when it was superseded by a structure variously described as 'the new drop in front of St George's fields'. This new gallows was trundled out into the open area in front of the Debtor's Prison, all the better to facilitate the multitudes of spectators who would crowd to watch an execution. And with the advent of the railway coming to York in the early 1840s, additional train services, or 'specials' as they were known, were laid on to better expediate the transport of the multitudes who would throng to the show of a public hanging.

There were of course less brutal forms of mass entertainment. Various fairs were held in York, the Candlemass Fair held on the Thursday before 25 February, on May Day, the Midsummer Fair held on 5 July and the Ringing Day fair on 5 November (the name of this fair alludes to the ringing of the bell hung in the marketplace on Pavement, which signified that trading was allowed to commence). While the sale of horses and cattle was the primary concern of all fairs, the last two fairs in the calendar were also pleasure fairs. Affording a kaleidoscope of sights and sounds, the fairs attracted entertainers such as rope dancers, tumblers and acrobats, with the addition of food stalls, fortune tellers, freak shows, and musicians playing hurdy-gurdys and fiddles, and of course the ubiquitous pickpockets and prostitutes were attendant at such gatherings.

While the presence and scale of prostitution in a seemingly genteel cathedral city such as York may seem surprising, as previously mentioned, the industrial boom that was building

A procuress recruits a prospective prostitute from Hogarth's 'A Harlot's Progress'.

up cities like Leeds, Bradford and Sheffield, offering employment opportunities for women as well as men, for the most part passed York by, and with the rapid population increase that began toward the latter part of the Georgian period, prostitution provided a means to an end for many (men and women) who were forced to utilise their bodies as a source of income.

The three Waters Lanes district of the city, prior to being swept away in the rush of Victorian development in the late 1880s, once occupied the area now covered by King Street, Cumberland Street and Clifford Street. It was then a collection of dark, overcrowded, filthy tenements and populated by those forced by circumstance into thieving and prostitution. Records indicate that certain areas of York, such as the central part of the walled city were concentrated centres for harlotry and brothels since the Middle Ages, long before the advent of the pressing needs of those crowded in the Water Lanes.

Today, Grape Lane, just a stone's throw from the Minster, linking Petergate with Swinegate, was once a dark alley called 'Grapecuntlane' – grape originally meaning to grope, the rest of the interpretation I leave to the reader and their own sensibilities! It was normal practice for medieval street names to reflect a street's once economic activity or function, and adjacent to Grape Lane is Finkle Street, a thoroughfare of similarly indecent and dubious reputation, which as late as the nineteenth century was still known as 'Murky (or Mucky) Peg' Lane.

Looking to more genteel diversions, the later Georgian era saw the invention of what we would term the 'shopping mall'. With the advent of plate glass windows up to a foot square replacing the bottle glass windows so beloved of the Dickensian imagination, shop owners could now show off their wares to better advantage; window-shopping became the new

Shopping for a hat, 1820.

pastime of both mistress and servant, even if the understairs maid were unable to afford those items that took her fancy. In turn, the light levels inside shops were much improved, and this meant that shoppers could now examine a potential purchase without having to go back out into the daylight of the street.

At this time, the retail trade was dominated by the independent merchant; there were no chain stores and each shop traded as they saw fit, though opening hours were dependent upon the rhythm of daylight hours. As a rule, grocers opened at dawn and stayed open until they had sold out for the day, or until dark. Most other shops would open at 8 a.m. and stay open until nightfall, or 9 p.m. in the summer months. The way that customers were looked after in larger establishments also provided useful on-the-job training for those employed in the retail sphere; as a customer browsed, they would be accompanied by an apprentice who would advocate the desirability and merits of each item for purchase. This allowed the apprentices to learn about the stock, and about the nature of retailing, as with Mary Tuke's nephew, William, who was apprenticed to her grocer's shop in Walmgate. This would also have served to help build clientele, developing a long-term customer relationship, and in turn the possibility of an astute apprentice even taking that custom with them if they set up in business themselves.

And York catered to every shopper's whim. In Stonegate alone there were a wide range of emporia, from the apothecary shop of Mr Palmer, Mrs Hopton's, where corsets might be purchased, and Thomas Hardy's outfitters, where one could buy gentlemen's breeches. John Todd's bookshop was at The Sign of the Bible (at this time it was usual for a shop to be identified by a visible sign of their trade, even those without premises to trade from utilised this method, freelance seamstresses often hanging out large wooden needles from their lodgings indicating their availability to work).

If Mr Todd didn't carry the book you were looking for, then John Wolstenholme also sold books at the corner of Petergate and Minster Gates – where the figure of Minerva can still be seen above the door casing. In common with most booksellers, he also sold other items – in his case, lottery tickets, sating the prevalent lust for gambling.

For the fashionable lady (and gent) seeking a diversity of silks and other costly fabrics, they might pay a visit to George Roe, silk mercer and linen draper, at the Sycamore in the Minster Yard, who in 1740,

> informs all persons – even those of the meanest capacity – that they can have the following goods either wholesale or retail, the prices being fixed without any abatement: Rich brocades in the newest patterns, Black and coloured Paduasoys, Velours and Tonquedells, Poplins, Superfine Broad Camblets, Tammils, Plodds, India Dermitties, Wrough Petticoats, Hair Prunelloes and Princess stuffs, and other goods too tedious to mention.

Milliners, dressmakers, haberdashers and wig makers also abounded; powder for hair (made from finely ground starch, scented with orange flower, lavender, or orris root, and occasionally colored blue, violet, pink or yellow, but most often white), and patches were beauty essentials for both sexes, although worn in proliferation by women, for the fashionable lady 'always had seven or eight [patches], and never went without her patch-box, so that she might put on more if she felt so inclined, or replace those that might happen to come off'. In fact, there was a secret language in the positioning of the patch as well as the functional aspect of disguising a rising pimple. Made from tiny pieces of black velvet, silk or taffeta (if you were poor you might have to make do with mouse's skin, also

'The Sign of the Bible', the original bookshop sign dating to 1682. (*Courtesy of The Evelyn Collection*)

York's Stonegate offered eighteenth-century shoppers a variety of retailers. (*Louise Rayner, courtesy of Harry Drummond, dudleymall.co.uk*)

The painted sculpture of Minerva still presides over the doorway of the premises that were Wolstenholme's bookshop.

employed in the manufacture of false eyebrows), patches were available in a myriad of precut shapes from hearts to crescent moons, and once affixed, with a mixture of glycerin and other ingredients including extract of sturgeon swim-bladder, placement could indicate the wearer's mood, or even political allegiance. At the corner of an eye indicated a passionate disposition; the middle of the cheek, the gallant; the nose, the impudent; near the mouth, the coquette, a patch on the forehead signified dignity; or around the lips, kissable. A bethrothed young woman wishing to announce her new status sported a heart on her left cheek. Upon her marriage she switched the heart to the right. And for those who wished to demonstrate their political affiliation, Whigs patched up to the right and Tories on the left!

In 1716, the desired look as described by Lady Mary Wortley Montagu was that 'All the ladies have ... snowy foreheads and bosoms, jet eyebrows and scarlet lips.' However, Georgian men as well as women coveted rouges, lipsticks and powders that would help them to attain the desired look. It was nevertheless an unfortunate consequence that the majority of cosmetics employed in this period contained toxic substances that could cumilatively prove fatal with prolonged use. As an example, many eighteenth-century rouges were made using the lead-base ingredient carmine, and applied to cheeks using bits of wet wool; the crimson cosmetic was also formulated into a lipstick by mixing it with plaster of Paris. The essential 'snowy' pallor alluded to by Lady Mary could be best achieved with a powder produced from finely flaked lead, with its attendant medical disadvantage of causing headaches, nausea, blindness or even death. At least achieving fashionable eyebrows proved less toxic, and presumably this is where the poor mouse's skin was employed if charcoal soot failed to produce the desired jet shade.

If the application of deadly cosmetics and shopping hadn't taken up the lion's share of the day, there was always the ritual of 'paying morning calls'. By the beginning of the

Leader of fashion, Madame du Pompadour, at her toilette, patch box in hand.

nineteenth century, the etiquette of calling was a firmly established practice in society. Bizarrely 'morning calls' were made in the afternoon, up to 4 p.m. Etiquette dictated that visits should be short, a stay from fifteen to twenty minutes being quite sufficient, good manners allowing the lady paying the visit to remove her boa or neckerchief, but never her shawl or bonnet, while tea was taken from fine porcelain cups.

While the ladies were busy visiting, the gentlemen might pass the afternoon in one of the fashionable coffee or chocolate houses, a vogue that had radiated from their initial establishment in the capital to the further reaches of outlying fashionable towns and cities. Patronised by the respectably dressed who would have paid an inclusive admission charge of one penny (this precluded the working man who would more usually frequent the tavern or ale house), along with a long clay pipe of tobacco provided by the management, a 'dish' of coffee or chocolate was proffered. Alternatively, sherbert (a chilled drink made from fruit juice sometimes effervesced with the addition of bicarbonate of soda) or less familiar today saloop, a drink made from the aromatic dried root of the sassafras, could be enjoyed while catching up on current affairs either by perusing the newspapers available to customers (the city's first newspaper, the *York Mercury* appeared on 23 February 1719, followed by many more over the succeeding decades), or listening to or participating with the general discussion, a conducive element to many frequenting such establishments. As well as the social aspect of such houses, they were also a useful places to conduct business, as well as, dare it be said, a haven from the company of women – saving for the female waiting staff, the fairer sex were not usually admitted.

No women patrons are depicted in Thomas Rowlandson's coffee house. However, the gentlemen customers are being comically terrorised by a 'mad dog' – a scene characteristic of the famous caricaturist's work.

For the working man there was always the ale house, and there was certainly plenty of choice. The *History, Directory & Gazetteer of Yorkshire* for 1823 lists 195 entries under inns and taverns in the City of York. These would have varied from bawdy houses serving liquor on the premises to the more respectable coaching inns. By 1796, three coaches ran daily from York to London, departing from the York Tavern in St Helen's Square and from the Black Swan on Coney Street, the inn's classical façade enlivened by a statue now displayed in York Castle Museum.

Alternatively, the theatre had long proved a popular entertainment. In 1744, York could enjoy the delights of the stage in the smart surroundings of the New Theatre opened by Mrs Kerrigan on the site of the current theatre in Mint Yard, built over and among the ruins of the medieval St Leonard's Hospital. The enterprising Mrs Kerrigan had taken on the theatre that had been opened by her husband on 1 October 1734, then located in Minster Yard. However, it was Tate Wilkinson, having taken over the management of the New Theatre in 1766, who was to be instrumental in the theatre's growing success, and with the granting of a Royal Patent in 1769, the New Theatre was renamed the Theatre Royal.

Theatre-going in the Georgian era was, however, a very different experience from that of today. Audiences could be noisy and rude, unruly and even dangerous if displeased by the performances. They chatted audibly among themselves, and sometimes pelted actors with rotten fruit and vegetables. Alcohol and food were freely consumed, with no stigma attached to arriving late or leaving mid-performance, amidst repeated demands that popular tunes be played over and over again.

Wilkinson's company was reckoned to be the leading provincial company, and he attracted many of the finest actors of the period, including John Philip Kemble, his sister Sarah Siddons and Elizabeth Farren, to act in York. Dorothea Jordan (long-standing mistress to the Duke of Clarence) appeared at the Theatre Royal in the summer of 1811. The publicity ran: 'Mrs Jordan is engaged for six nights and will make her appearance on Thursday, August 1, in her celebrated character of The Country Girl'. It was on an earlier visit to York that Dora Bland had adopted the stage name and change in marital status in a bid to add a touch of respectability to her growing fame.

While Mrs Jordan may well have proved a box office draw, having wooed London audiences in the role, the cost to theatre-goers was not cheap – a box cost 4*s*, while a seat downstairs would set you back 2*s* 6*d*.

A cheaper alternative might be to go and see the circus, which made periodic visits to the city – in September 1811, the circus pitched just outside Bootham included tightrope dancing as well as a 'Cotillion with Six Horses', presumably the spectacle involving some equine dance steps. Another notable thrill was Madame Tussaud and her travelling exhibition. After an invitation to visit London in 1802, the founder of the famous wax museum, finding herself unable to return to her native France because of the Napoleonic Wars, travelled throughout Great Britain and Ireland exhibiting her collection. On coming to York, her 'Grand European Cabinet of Figures Consisting of sixty-nine public characters modelled from life' could be viewed in Goodramgate from 10 a.m. until 11 p.m. at night,

Box office draw Mrs Jordan played the Theatre Royal, York.

admission 1s, children admitted half price. There was also a collection of 'curiosities' to be wondered at the Sycamore Tree, Minster Yard, though Jane Ewbank, daughter of a local Anglican clergyman recorded in her journal for 13 February 1804 that after visiting the collection that 'the only thing worth notice is a young crocodile brought alive from Egypt'.

Then as now, a royal visit always drew a crowd. Though various monarchs over the ages had dipped in and out of the city on the course of a royal northern progress, there had not been a royal wedding in York since 1327, when Edward III married Philippa of Hainault, the ceremony conducted in the teeth of a violent snowstorm as the Minister was unfinished at the time, the roofless nave offering no protection from the blizzard raging outside. The closest York came to a coronation was the investiture of Richard III's son, Edward of Middleham, as Prince of Wales, the ceremony performed at the Archbishop's Palace behind the Minster in 1483.

Royal visits to York in the Georgian period were sporadic, and often short. In 1746, the Duke of Cumberland (Prince William, a younger son of George II) visited the city after his crushing defeat of the Jacobite rebellion at Culloden. Twenty-two of the rebels were executed at York, and two of the traitor's heads were still on display spiked above Micklegate Bar at the time of his visit – presumably to the satisfaction of 'Butcher Cumberland'.

The next royal visit wasn't until 1761, when Prince Edward, Duke of York, was received by the city with 'great ceremony'. On 31 August 1768, King Christian VII of Denmark extended his UK visit to York, but his majesty remained only two days. The year 1789 saw the return of the Duke of York, in the company of his brother, future George IV, both come to attend the York Races, and in November 1795 Prince William, Duke of Gloucester, paid a visit to the city on his return from Scarborough. It wasn't until 1820 that York was graced with a further royal presence – Prince Leopold, latterly King of the Belgians and widower of Princess Charlotte of Wales, the only child of George IV, who had died in childbirth three years previously.

Other illustrious personages to grace York with their presence were the Earl St Vincent, received in York in 1805, a patron of Horatio Nelson, the Earl being best known for his

Plaque on the wall of the old palace, behind the Minster, commemorating Edward of Middleham's investiture.

Gillray's satirical portrayal of the Prince of Wales, later Prince Regent and George IV.

victory over the Spanish (allied to Napoleonic France) in the 1797 Battle of Cape Saint Vincent, from which the Earl earned his title. And in September 1827, York welcomed the victor of Waterloo; the Duke of Wellington was 'received with the greatest enthusiasm a grateful people could evince, for the eminent services he had rendered his country.

While these distinguished dignitaries may well have been cheered through the streets, there were those, of a satirical bent, who would have enjoyed with equal measure the derision and ridicule such personages received at the hands of the great caricaturists of the day. Relaxation in the censorship laws meant that royalty, politicians and the rich and famous personalities were all ripe targets for the lampooning works of Gillray, Cruickshank and Rowlandson – the follies of everyday life also came under satirical scrutiny, Rowlandson's parody of 'Execution Day in York' and 'A Mad Dog in a Coffee-House' pictured earlier in this chapter are both apt examples.

And critics of the twenty-first-century culture of celebrity obsession needn't think the taste for scandal is anything new. Plenty of the Georgian publications are still going strong today, including the *Tatler*, founded in 1709, the *Spectator* (1711) and the *Observer* (1791), they, then as now, promoted feverish public interest in the great figures of the day. Not only were political personalities and military heroes of the moment subject to scrutiny, but the antics of the scandalous beauties of the day also drew avid attention, such as Nelson's lover Lady Hamilton, and leading courtesan of her day, Kitty Fisher, a consummate self-promoter who commissioned the celebrated artist Joshua Reynolds to paint her portrait so that prints could be sold to her legion of admirers.

How little things have changed...

5

A Question of Belief

It is indisputable that some of the most famous names in chocolate were Quakers, who for centuries held a virtual monopoly over chocolate manufacture in the English-speaking world – Rowntree's and Terrys held sway in York, while Fry's grew to prominence in Bristol and Cadbury dominated production in Birmingham.

A number of factors contributed to the Quaker gravitation toward the chocolate industry. However, the predominant reason lay with their ethical reaction against the

Adriaen Brouwer's depiction of drunkenness sums up the prevalent problem of alcohol abuse, long endemic in the lower classes of society.

attendant distress and deprivation caused by the excessive consumption of alcohol in the eighteenth and nineteenth centuries. As part of the Temperance Movement, along with other non-conformists, Quakers shared concerns about the extent of alcohol misuse commonplace in the population at large, but particularly the detrimental effects to those in the lower classes of society.

Cocoa presented an inexpensive and available substitute to alcohol, with the added health advantage that it was necessary to boil the water first, a definite plus in an era of poor public health and suspect water supply. Marketed as 'more than a drink a food', cocoa challenged the idea that consumption of beer was essential to a manual worker because drinking chocolate gave him sustenance as well as refreshment.

The Quaker Movement also possessed specific advantages, which aided their progress in business and gave them a distinctly competitive edge, namely their reputation for honesty and reliability. Quakers were among the first to set a firm price for goods rather than the usual practice of bartering with the customer; their stated prices also being fair prices, a part of the Quaker ethic that maintaining a livelihood should not come at the expense or exploitation of customers or employees – the welfare of the latter becoming a paramount concern as we shall see later.

Quakers gained a further advantage in the retail market through their ethical approach in their refusal to adulterate any foodstuffs. Contrary to prevalent practice in a climate where contamination, particularly of sweets, was a big issue, Quaker confectioners were trusted not to adulterate their products as a matter of conscience. The rather more unscrupulous manufacturers were adding red lead as a colouring for sweets (which incidentally was poisonous), brick dust and wax found its way into chocolate, used dried tea leaves were added to new, sand was put in coffee and starch powder added to cream; all helped to underhandedly expand on the profit margin.

The strength of networking among Quakers was also a decided benefit, bourne as it was from their strong sense of comradeship, a response to their exclusion and persecution in a religiously intolerant society. Known to one another through their church-based life, personal as well as business networks were firmly rooted.

As certain spheres of business were closed off as a direct result of their beliefs, Quakers were consequently driven toward trade and commerce as a direct result of their adherence to their faith. As confirmed pacifists, a career in the military was ruled out, and as non-conformists, they were excluded from universities (only practising Anglicans could take a degree), thus precluding professions such as the law and, of course, those within the established church. In addition, the refusal of Quakers to swear any oath – based on the interpretation of Matthew 5:34–37 – also barred them from many public or civic offices.

To better understand the social and commercial discrimination applied to the Quakers, we should perhaps go back to their formation as a splinter movement of dissenting Protestant groups who began to break away from the established Church of England in the mid-seventeenth century; an action that resulted in their persecution and exclusion to the edge of society.

The Quaker movement began as an offshoot of the Puritans, themselves a pacifist movement who were the product of the growing discontent within the established church, and who sought to strip away the traditional trappings and formalities of Christianity that had been slowly crystallising over the previous 1,500 years. Puritans advocated the purification of the church as well as of their own lives, at the same time working towards religious, moral and societal reform. Though the Puritans became a major political force in England as a result of the English Civil War (1642–46), after the Restoration of the

A broadsheet of 1647, cataloguing 'the Severall Sects and Opinions in England and other Nations: With a briefe Rehearsall of their false and dangerous Tenents'.

monarchy in 1660 and the Uniformity Act passed in 1662, prescribing adherence to the doctrine of the Established Church of England, Puritan ascendancy waned. As a result, the concept of non-conformity was created, and subsequent sub-groups formed, one of which was the Religious Society of Friends, a collective movement of which the Quakers, or Friends, were and are members.

These Quakers attempted to convert others to their understanding of Christianity, travelling throughout Great Britain and overseas, preaching the gospel of Jesus Christ. Some of the early Quaker ministers were even women, and this in itself was an anathema to the deeply entrenched patriarchal society of the seventeenth century. The Quaker message was simple and based upon the belief that 'Christ has come to teach his people himself', the pivotal factor being that of a direct relationship with God through Jesus Christ, and a personal and direct religious experience of Christ, acquired through both direct religious experience and the reading and studying of the Bible. Quakers saw no necessity for paid ministers, with prayer meetings held in silence, broken only when a member felt moved to speak or offer a prayer, a form of worship known as 'spoken ministry'. And it was this unassailable belief that a direct experience of Christ was possible without the aid of ordained clergy that so inflamed the established church, and landed George Fox, founder of the Quaker movement, in so much trouble.

Fox's uncompromising approach to the Christian faith pitted him against the religious and political authorities alike. Driven by his 'inner voice' Fox had been preaching publicly since 1647, sometimes at appointed meetings, otherwise in marketplaces, fields, and even utilising 'steeple-houses' after the Sunday service was over. His powerful preaching began to attract a small but significant following, and in 1650, Fox appeared before the magistrates in Derby on a charge of religious blasphemy. It was during this hearing when the judge mocked

Fox's exhortation to him to 'tremble at the word of the Lord' that the term 'Quakers' was first used. In 1651, George Fox had travelled to York, arriving two days before 'the time called Christmas' to quote the terminology of his autobiography. Fox further relates how he was

> commanded of the Lord to go and speak to priest Bowles and his hearers in their great cathedral. Accordingly I went. When the priest had done, I told them I had something from the Lord God to speak to the priest and people. 'Then say on quickly,' said a professor, for there was frost and snow, and it was very cold weather. Then I told them that this was the Word of the Lord God unto them, -- that they lived in words, but God Almighty looked for fruits among them. As soon as the words were out of my mouth, they hurried me out, and threw me down the steps. But I got up again without hurt, and went to my lodging...

Fox was lucky in this instance to have just ended up with a bruised rump. He was to be imprisoned several times in his spiritual career, firstly in Nottingham gaol in 1649 and a spell in prison at Derby after the blasphemy trial mentioned earlier. One of Fox's earliest converts in the county of York, Thomas Aldam, was also to suffer imprisonment; he was among the first of many Quakers detained in York Castle for their religious principles. Adlam

George Fox, founder of the Religious Society of Friends, commonly known as the Quakers or Friends.

remained a prisoner for about two and a half years, during which time his wife and family were frequently denied visiting rights. During this confinement, Aldam was brought before Judge Parker, and as he declined to remove his hat on conscientious motives and insisted on addressing the judge as 'thee' instead of 'you'. Aldam's conduct cost him dearly and he was fined £40 and committed to prison until such time as the fine was paid. However, on application to Oliver Cromwell, the Lord Protector granted an order for Adlam's liberation. Yet the persecutions continued. Following the Restoration in 1660, in just two months 535 Friends from York and Yorkshire were imprisoned in York Castle Gaol. The following year saw a further mass imprisonment of sixty-six Wakefield Friends, who went to York Castle rather than take an oath of conformity to the established church, as this would have been contrary to their conscience. No surprise then that according to Joseph Besse's *A Collection of the Sufferings of the People Called Quakers,* he records that in York Castle 'five of the [Quaker] prisoners died through the unhealthiness of the Place, where they were thronged together'. In fact, Mary Tuke's grandfather, William, was twice imprisoned during this period for his adherence to Quakerism (he was at the time a blacksmith in Walmgate), fortunately he was not held in the castle but in one of the city kidcotes, small lockups of which several existed – William was detained in the 'Sheriff's Prison', the gaol beneath the chapel that used to stand on the old Ouse Bridge. While William Tuke survived imprisonment, his property was confiscated because of his religious beliefs.

It would be over 150 years before prison conditions were addressed, and it was the Quaker Elizabeth Fry, depicted on the Bank of England £5 note, and sometimes referred to as the 'angel of prisons', who was instrumental in attempts to improve the appalling conditions inside prisons and a driving force behind new legislation to make the treatment of prisoners more humane.

However, Fry was not alone among Quaker social reformers – William Tuke, nephew of 'Mother of Chocolate' Mary Tuke, in tandem with running the successfully expanding family grocery business, also became known as a leading Quaker philanthropist, spearheading the introduction of new, more humane methods of caring for the mentally ill. The establishment of the York Retreat was a direct development of Quaker reaction to the harsh and inhumane 'treatments' usually employed in asylums of that era. The catalyst for William Tuke's involvement was the death of a Quaker woman named Hannah Mills in 1790. Hannah, a young widow from Leeds, was admitted to the York County Lunatic Asylum on 15 March suffering from 'melancholy' – in all probability clinical depression – but by 29 April, less than seven weeks later, she was dead. Local York Quakers had attempted to visit Hannah during her incarceration at the request of her relatives back in Leeds. However, visiting permission was refused on the grounds that Hannah was undergoing 'private treatment'. Concerns and suspicions about conditions and the 'treatments' at the York asylum were confirmed when a visit was finally permitted, revealing the shocking circumstances in which patients were kept and treated, with reports that those receiving care were treated 'worse than animals'. Recommended and widespread medical practices for treatment of the insane at this time included debilitating purges, painful blistering, long-term immobilisation in manacles chained to the wall, as well as sudden immersion in freezing cold baths. Quaker therapeutic beliefs, however, ran in total variance to the existing regimes administered in a climate of fear and brutality. Subsequent to the horrors revealed at York Asylum, William Tuke was enlisted to take charge of a project to develop a new form of asylum and take the lead in Quaker efforts to develop a more humane approach to the care of the mentally ill.

Tuke's method was one of direct appeal for funds made to fellow Quakers, to physicians as well as his own personal acquaintances. During the two years Tuke spent in discussion with the York Monthly Meeting (York's local Quaker group) outlining the fundamental principles of the proposed institution, he, along with his personal physician Timothy Maud, undertook to educate themselves as to the current thoughts and modes in the treatment of 'madness'. The upshot of this exercise was Tuke's overriding conviction in the importance of a benevolent and comfortable environment in which reflection could be encouraged.

As an alternative to the York County Lunatic Asylum, The Retreat opened in 1796, in the then countryside outside York, a mile from the city centre in the Lamel Hill area, off the Heslington Road. Gone were the physical restraints, and all physical punishment was banned. Treatment was now based on restoration of self-esteem and self-control, and while some minimal use of restraint was still necessary, door locks were now encased in leather, the bars to the windows were made to look like ordinary frames, and the extensive gardens included a sunken wall that though impassable was barely visible. Straitjackets were a last resort. An early form of occupational therapy was also introduced, patients encouraged to wander freely around The Retreat's courtyards and gardens, which were stocked with various small domestic animals; in these quiet and pleasant surroundings a treatment regimen based on personalised attention, kindness, moderation, order and trust was followed, alongside a religious component that included prayer.

William Tuke was also involved in the founding, in 1779, of a boarding school – the Ackworth School – for Quaker boys and girls in High Ackworth near Pontefract, along with fellow Quaker philanthropist John Fothergill. Further assisting with the founding of the Trinity Lane Quaker Girls' School in York in 1785, the precursor to The Mount School, Tuke also put forward the idea of another boarding school for Quaker boys in 1818, who were not eligible to attend the Ackworth School. In 1822 premises in the city on Lawrence Street were leased from The Retreat, the Bootham School opening in 1823.

The Retreat, *c.* 1796.

Maintaining the family philanthropic convictions, William's son Henry and grandson Samuel were instrumental in advocating the pioneering approach to mental health practiced at The Retreat. Though the new methods had at first been widely derided by the medical fraternity at large, thanks to the publicising efforts of the Tukes, The Retreat was eventually acknowledged as a model for effective treatment of those suffering psychological disorders. A successive generation of Tuke's carried on the good work, Samuel's son James Hack Tuke in his turn assisted with the management of The Retreat (later focusing his efforts on famine relief aid to Ireland). James's brother Daniel Hack Tuke co-wrote the important treatise *A Manual of Psychological Medicine*, published in 1858, and became a leading physician dedicated to the study of mental illness.

Samuel Tuke shared his philanthropic views and ideas almost daily with friend and fellow Quaker Joseph Rowntree (Senior), whose family were of course to later take on the chocolate manufacturing side of the Tuke's then business that, in Samuel's day, also comprised a tea dealership. The relative successes of Samuel's and Joseph Senior's businesses enabled them both to devote their time and focus their energies on the pressing social issues of the day, and in 1832, Tuke and Rowntree founded the Friends Provident Institution in Bradford, a friendly society that was the first investment house in the UK to offer a fully ethical investment fund.

Joseph Rowntree was certainly not remiss in indelibly impressing his social scruples upon his sons either. In 1848, John and Joseph Junior (then aged sixteen and fourteen) were taken to Ireland by their father to experience first-hand the dire consequences of a famine-stricken people, whose poverty had been exacerbated by the British government's failure to earlier take mitigating measures.

Perhaps those three weeks spent in Ireland, during which Joseph Junior was exposed to the horrors and the desperations of the dying, and those already dead heaped into mass graves, had a lasting effect on the young man and engendered his later establishment of the garden village of New Earswick. It provided better housing for people on low incomes as an alternative to the dark, overcrowded and insanitary conditions they were ordinarily forced to live in.

Prior to this endeavour, however, in York in the mid-Victorian era, it was a statistically deplorable fact that one man in five and one woman in three could neither read nor write. In 1857, the York Quakers had been instrumental in converting a woodturner's shop in Lady Peckett's Yard into the first adult school, and through scripture lessons, Joseph and his brothers John and Henry Isaac, along with other Quakers, helped to teach illiterate men, and later women, to read and write. It was during this period that Joseph really learnt of the difficulties and the privations of the lives of the poor of York first-hand.

A forerunner to Rowntree's New Earswick was the creation of fellow Quaker industrialist brothers George and Richard Cadbury's development of Bourneville – their 'Factory in a Garden' initially occupying a 14-acre greenfield site, 4 miles from the heart of industrial Birmingham.

The Cadburys were appalled by the conditions of penury and squalor in which the workers of the city subsisted. Labouring for a pittance in the factories, those lured in by the false promise of higher wages returned at night to overcrowded accommodation with all the attendant problems arising from densely populated slums.

In 1879, George Cadbury and his brother Richard took the decision to take the signal socially ethical stand to move their successful chocolate manufacturing business away from the noxiously polluted surroundings of industrial Birmingham to a site in the open countryside outside of the city. The objectives were quite clear – an estate comprising of

Above left: Samuel Tuke.

Above right: Daniel Hack Tuke.

Right: Joseph Rowntree's first-hand experience of the extreme privations of Irish famie victims may well have engendered his later philanthropic approach to the plight of York's poor.

decent quality homes at prices within the reach of the industrial workers, 'intended to make it easy for working men to own houses with large gardens, secure from the dangers of being spoilt either by factories, or by the interference with the enjoyment of sun, light and air'.

Joseph Rowntree's New Earswick then echoed Cadbury's conspicuous contribution to the sphere of later Victorian social reforms (not forgetting of course the establishment of Saltaire in 1851 and Port Sunlight in 1888). In 1901, Joseph's son Seebohm Rowntree, who had entered the family cocoa and chocolate business in 1889 when he was eighteen years old, published a study of the living conditions of the working classes in York. Entitled 'Poverty: a study of town life', Seebohm's research revealed shocking statistics that affirmed the reality of dark, overcrowded and insanitary housing conditions.

The same year that Seebohm published his study, Joseph Rowntree's conviction that it must be possible to provide better housing for people on low incomes led him to acquire 150 acres of land near the village of Earswick, 2½ to the north of the centre of York. This new 'garden' village was created with the intention of engendering a balanced community where, although rents were to be kept low, they should still represent a modest commercial return on the capital invested, and not restricted to just Rowntree employees, with the new housing open to any working people. With raw materials sourced from the brickworks on the outskirts of the village, Rowntree's hope was that if New Earswick were a success, with dwellings that had gardens with fruit trees and enough ground to grow vegetables, that similar communities would be built elsewhere in the country.

Aerial photograph of Joseph Rowntree's New Earswick. (*Courtesy of The Evelyn Collection*)

Joseph Rowntree further provided a library and free education for all workers under the age of seventeen, and a social welfare officer, doctor and a dentist were employed to provide free services for the workforce. With longer term welfare in mind, Joseph Rowntree also donated £10,000 in 1906 to establish a pension fund for his workers, though one of his main and instantly impactful innovations was to give the workers a say in the appointment of their immediate supervisors.

Indeed, both New Earswick and Bourneville continue to be a thriving communities today, with their respective trusts ensuring the continuation of the founding ethics, and influencing the development of the later garden cities of Letchworth and Welwyn Garden City.

Joseph Rowntree also endowed a legacy of trusts that are still in operation today, as well as the Joseph Rowntree Foundation, which funds a UK-wide research and development programme, the goal of which is to inspire social change. The Joseph Rowntree Reform Trust aims to correct imbalances of political power, strengthening the hands of individuals and organisations striving for reform; The Joseph Rowntree Charitable Trust continues to make available grants to promote peace, equality and accountability, echoing the spirit of New Earswick; while The Joseph Rowntree Housing Trust administers a registered housing association, managing around 2,500 homes in Yorkshire and the North East.

With regard to the other improving Quaker legacies, namely those of the Tukes, The Retreat still endures, providing care for the mentally ill, an offshoot of which is The Tuke Centre, specialising in psychotherapy and counselling, and the Bootham and Mount Schools still maintain their Quaker ethos.

The York Friends Meeting House in Friargate, first built in 1674, and where Joseph Rowntree is known to have attended, still holds regular meetings. Though the building has undergone several redevelopments since, at its height it had a large gallery and could accommodate up to 1,200 people; the fact that there were several institutions and businesses in York that were Quaker-led helped to underpin and strengthen the growth of Quakerism in York.

Another poignant reminder of York's Quaker past can be found in the Society of Friends burial ground at Bishophill, now tucked away in a peaceful garden behind some residential flats, to one side of Carrs Lane. Here, marked with very plain and small round-topped headstones giving only the name, age and date of death, lay some of the Tukes under the turf of this the first Quaker burial ground in York, purchased in 1667 by John Woolman, a friend of Benjamin Franklin and early advocate of the abolition of slavery; he also lies buried there.

In a chapter concerning the influence of Quakerism, and those York Quakers who were the cornerstones of the City's confectionery industry, it would be pertinent to mention their stance, personally and from a business point of view, with regards to war.

One of the pillars of Quaker belief is that war and conflict are against God's wishes. Taking the practical point of view that force nearly always creates more problems than it solves, Quakers are dedicated to pacifism and non-violence.

As early as 1660, a Quaker statement made to King Charles II affirmed 'We utterly deny all outward wars and strife and fightings with outward weapons, for any end or under any pretence whatsoever, and this is our testimony to the whole world.'

For Quaker industrialists like Rowntree and Cadbury, national embroilment in the Boer War (1899–1902) served to unite their strong opposition, especially in the face of the inhumanity of British concentration camps in South Africa (not, as generally supposed, a Nazi concept). In 1900, George Cadbury incurred royal displeasure when he refused to furnish British troops with 120,000 tins of chocolate on account of his ethical beliefs. However, when Queen Victoria indicated that her's was not a request but a royal command, Cadbury was obliged to comply. Ultimately, an arrangement was reached by sharing production with

Bootham School. Today this co-educational, independent school for pupils aged three to eighteen still maintains the Quaker ethos on which it was founded, and welcomes all faiths and backgrounds.

Friargate Quaker Meeting House.

Bishophill Quaker Burial Ground. Quakers, Chocolate and War…

Frank J. Stevens, a Friends Ambulance Unit ambulance driver, with his vehicle in Wolfsburg, Germany, during the Second World War.

The Haxby Road War Memorial dedicated to the memory of those chocolate workers who gave their lives in both World Wars.

fellow Quaker manufacturers Rowntree and Fry's of Bristol, the tins in which the chocolate was contained as devoid of all branding, thus ameliorating their collective conscience.

With the outbreak of the First World War in 1914, the Lord Mayor of York, himself free of ethical constraints, sent a bar of Rowntree's chocolate to every soldier fighting in the Great War, and one of the original tins with the chocolate bar still inside is on display in The Mansion House.

However, with the advent of mass drafting and the Military Service Bill introduced in January 1916, providing for the conscription of single men aged eighteen to forty-one (in May of that year extended to married men), the problem of conscientious objection raised its head; those conscripted men adhering to their Quaker principles refused to take up arms. Initially, Rowntree refused to comply with the policy of dismissing conscientious objectors from his workforce, but by 1916 the company ceased employment of objectors on the grounds that their presence in the workforce generated animosity. Joseph's nephew, Arnold Stephenson Rowntree, as a Quaker and Liberal MP for the York, championed the cause of the city's conscientious objectors, making the most of his position to highlight the cause of those who refused to fight. Unfortunately, he was unable to prevent the death of Alfred Martlew, a clerk at Rowntrees and a committed Quaker, who was so deeply distressed by his enforced conscription in France that he took his own life; he was found drowned in the River Ouse on 11 July 1917, the newspaper article simply stated 'An Objector Drowned'. Arnold Stephenson Rowntree was, however, successful in his efforts to establish the Friends Ambulance Unit, a volunteer group that ferried casualties from the front line, allowing conscientious objectors to contribute to the war effort without being involved in direct combat; the unit operated in the Second World War also.

Tensions remained high after the war was over, and many conscientious objectors found it hard to gain employment. Arnold continued to use his influence within the family business, and as chairman of the management committee at The Retreat hospital, assisted many objectors back into work.

During the Second World War, in the face of manpower restrictions and the shortage of raw materials and rationing, the Rowntree factories were temporarily converted to assist with the war effort. Much of Rowntree's office block on Haxby Road was given over to the Royal Army pay corps, and the cream department was reconfigured for the production of munitions, while the gum department was covertly renamed County Industries and converted into a secret fuse factory.

In memory of those who had fallen in both conflicts, Rowntree Park, donated by Joseph Rowntree at the end of the First World War was created as a memorial to all those employees of Rowntree's who died in the First World War, while the gates at the riverbank entrance to the park were given by the company as a memorial to all those people of York who died in the Second World War.

Chocolate workers from York who gave their lives for their country are also remembered with a war memorial given pride of place during Nestlé's redevelopment of the entrance to its Haxby Road site, honouring workers from Nestlé's predecessor Rowntree. The names of those who died in the First and Second World Wars are commemorated on replicas of plaques originally displayed in the Rowntree dining room, now part of the Nuffield Hospital situated opposite Rowntree's former factory.

Today, the Joseph Rowntree Charitable Trust remains committed to a culture of peace and the creation of a peaceful world, supporting work that promotes non-violent conflict resolution, with focus on the arms trade, development of effective peace-building measures and supporting the right to conscientious objection to military service.

6

Chocolate City Then and Now

Certainly the confectionery industry that grew from one woman's commercial endeavour in the Georgian era created a lifelong heritage for York and its people, and the city's claim to the title of Britain's official home of chocolate is an entirely justifiable one.

After all, the industry was responsible for assuring the economic stability of York in the nineteenth century and beyond, and while there may not be so much left of the original confectionery names of Rowntree, Terry and Craven, confectionery still plays an important role in York, a status maintained by the continuance and scale of manufacture. After the 1988 acquisition of Rowntree, Nestlé remains the largest private employer in the city.

Considering the context in which York's involvement with chocolate began, and the mighty commercial concern the industry occupies today, indeed from little acorns mighty oaks do grow. From the beginnings of Mary Tuke's great enterprise in opening her grocer's shop in Walmgate in 1725, York's Nestlé Rowntree factory is now one of the world's largest confectionery production sites (with the mouthwatering production of over a billion Kit Kats a year) and is also home to the global centre for confectionery research and development at the Nestlé Product Technology Centre.

While to hypothesise about the convergence of contributory factors might lead one down the road of 'what ifs', it remains a fact that of the ten 'confectioners' listed as trading in the City of York in the *History, Directory & Gazetteer of Yorkshire* for 1823 (the majority of whose businesses were clustered around what we still regard as the centre of the city, between the Shambles and the Minster), three would go on to become recognisable household names.

Indeed, had York's eighteenth-century story been one of industrial success, uninhibited as it was by the conspiring hinderance of geographical and economic factors, the conversant of which proved so beneficial to booming cities such as Leeds, Manchester and Hull, the emergence and existence of the confectionery capital might never have been. The dolorous status of York in comparison with its industrially successful neighbours was the catalyst for the establishment of a city replete with the social ideals of polite and cultured society so prized by the Hanoverian elite, and provided the impetus behind the city's Georgian prosperity. Thanks to the rise in the climate of conspicuous consumption in the Second City, York's urban renaissance was directly attributable to the demand for opulence, spawning a plethora of businesses catering to the needs of the affluent, and assuring its revival as a

Nestlé, Haxby Road.

regional metropolis, where the dynamic element in the city's economy was the pursuit of luxury, one of which was of course was the consumption of chocolate.

Of course, Quakerism was another integral factor in the shaping of 'Chocolate City'; the presence of a core of Quaker citizens underpinned York's development as a city of business. With the preclusion of members of The Society of Friends from entering certain spheres of economic activity (nonconformists being excluded from professions such as the military, established church, and the law), they were instead driven toward trade and commerce, and chocolate and Quakers made natural partners. With their ethical reaction against the attendant distress and deprivation caused by alcohol in the eighteenth and nineteenth centuries, the development and production of chocolate as a substitute to the massive consumption of beer thought necessary to sustain the energies of the working classes was a primary goal of Quaker chocolte manufacturers.

As we have seen, the chocolate industry shaped York as a city, both socially and economically, the rise and establishment of such providing employment and succour throughout the heyday of confectionery production. For example, in 1851, when Joseph Terry Junior joined his father's business, the workforce numbered 127. Coupled with

Rowntree Elect Cocoa advert. (*Courtesy of Brian Elsey*)

Craven's employment of sixty-three men and sixty boys, the confectionery industry was the second largest employer in York at that time. Between 1883 and 1894, the number of Rowntree employees rose from 200 to 894, the introduction of Rowntree's Elect Cocoa in 1887 primarily responsible for the company's growth. Within eight years, the output of Elect Cocoa had risen from 16 hundredweight a year to 26 tons, necessitating the move to the more expansive premises of the purpose-built factory on the Haxby Road site. By 1906, Rowntree's employee numbers had swelled to 4,066.

Competing in the employment stakes, by 1895 Terry's workforce had increased to 300 employees, after the move from the St Helen's Square premises to the new, steam-powered chocolate factory at Clementhorpe in 1886. However, by the time of the royal visit of King George VI and Queen Mary in 1937 – marked by the production of a special 'King George Assortment' and a 'Coronation Assortment' – Terry's had then moved to even more expansive premises on Bishopthorpe Road, near the Knavesmire racecourse. The employee count had risen to 2,500, some 60 per cent of whom were women, and 300 of these were employed in the offices or as sales representatives. This new factory, built in 1927, was designed in line with the latest ideas on factory architecture and equipment – the iconic 135-foot clock tower soaring above the boiler house based on the design of the front of the Woolworth building in New York. Sadly, this grand entrance, once flanked with the firm's logo of twin palm trees, born of Terry's purchase of a cocoa plantation in the Venezuelan Andes, is now boarded up, the factory silent after Terry's closed its doors for the last time

View of Terry's Clementhorpe factory seen from across the river. (*Courtesy of The Evelyn Collection*)

Terry's advertisement, featuring Clementhorpe Works bottom right. (*Courtesy of Brian Elsey*)

on 30 September 2005. In this respect, we should perhaps examine the path leading to the somewhat eclipsed industry as it exists today.

By the turn of the twentieth century, UK chocolate manufacturers were facing the challenge from foreign producers who were increasingly dominating the domestic market in view of the rising popularity of milk chocolate. Van Houten were a rival Dutch concern who, in the 1860s, were the only manufacturer to possess the secret of a press that could extract extraneous cocoa butter essential to the production of eating chocolate; they had also perfected an alkalising essence that modified the colour of chocolate and also gave their product a milder taste. With UK sales agencies in London, Leeds, Liverpool, Edinburgh and Glasgow, Van Houten presented a strong commercial threat alongside the Swiss producers Maison Cailler, who were at the time the leaders in producing milk chocolate.

In spite of Joseph Rowntree's somewhat deluded belief that the demand for milk chocolate was nothing more than a passing craze, Rowntree did make an early attempt at competing in this increasingly lucrative market with the introduction of their first milk chocolate block. However, instead of following the Swiss manufacturing style of using condensed, powdered milk in production. 'Rowntree's Swiss Milk Chocolate' was not a success. As the Swiss tightened their hold on the milk chocolate market, between 1904 (that year Nestlé had started importing milk chocolate to the UK) and 1910, Rowntree made further attempts to break into the milk chocolate market with 'Mountain Milk Chocolate', 'Alpine Milk Chocolate' and 'Malted Milk Chocolate'. However, all met with failure.

From the 1850s, Van Houten were forerunners in marketing and PR, another area in which they eclipsed Rowntree, until the company's revision of their advertising policy in the 1920s. (*Courtesy of Grace's Guide*)

Rowntree was further hobbled by their governing belief that there would always be a healthy market for the best goods it could produce – the measure of quality determined within the company and not necessarily by the consumer. In hindsight, this belief, bolstered by the company's commercial success in the nineteenth century, was in the long term to prove detrimental to sales. With no emphasis on research, products were developed with scant knowledge of consumer desires and very little consideration given to potential market profitability. Marketing was further hampered by the company doctrine concerning advertising – in line with the Quaker belief that if the quality of a product was good enough this should be sufficient to encourage purchase, Joseph Rowntree was also strongly opposed to advertising. Suspicious of press and poster campaigns, his ethics were further reinforced by the often false claims promoted by many advertisers before the advent of consumer protection against such misleading marketing.

After Seebohm Rowntree succeeded his father as chairman in February 1923 (Joseph Rowntree died on 24 February 1925). Despite the Rowntree board's final acceptance that advertising would be the most attainable way to turn around the company's fortunes, the cumulative effects of poor past marketing, and the considerable loss of market share to domestic competitor Cadbury, who in 1919 had merged with Fry's of Bristol, meant that the company's prospects looked bleak. This was compounded by the 1929 Wall Street Crash, and by 1930 Rowntree was brought to the edge of bankruptcy.

But all was not lost. The eventual decline in the dominance of foreign importers, sweeping changes in the integration of departments and changes to the constitution of the board (all

Rowntree Black Magic advertisement. (*Courtesy of Grace's Guide*)

directors would hence be working executives) helped rescue Rowntree from the financial doldrums in which the company found itself adrift. Renowned advertising agents J. Walter Thompson (responsible for Cadbury's 'glass and a half' branding) also came on board, along with the dynamic and hard-working new sales manager, George Harris (who would rise to become future chairman). From Harris' recognition that Rowntree's future success depended on consumer marketing and branding in a climate of intense competition, the 1930s saw the launch of Kit Kat, Aero and Smarties, and also the introduction of higher end boxed assortments like Dairy Box and Black Magic.

However, with the advent of the Second World War, these assortments were the first of Rowntree's casualties. Import of raw materials dwindled, domestic milk supply was diverted and with the introduction of chocolate rationing in 1942, consumption restricted to 3 ounces per person per week (less than half the pre-war average), inevitably the result was reduced production. Though the majority of the Rowntree production sites were fortunate enough to escape the Luftwaffe bombardment of industrial targets, in 1942 the warehouse on North Street was razed. By the time the war came to a close in 1945, Rowntree's sales were halved. In 1948, a further blow had been dealt by a viral disease carried by the mealybug, accounting for the decimation of 16 per cent of the world cocoa-producing plantations.

But with the cessation of rationing in 1953, the state of economic privation was alleviated, and 1954 saw a peak in UK confectionary consumption. Rowntree also took advantage of the advertising opportunities presented by the launch of commercial television in 1955, and by 1958, 60 per cent of Rowntree's advertising budget was given over to television commercials, one such successful campaign supporting the launch of the 'After Eight Thin Mint' in 1962. By 1966, Rowntree's share of the UK confectionery business was 15 per cent, with Kit Kat accounting for 20 per cent of all Rowntree revenue. Then, in 1969, Rowntree's merged with Mackintosh's, and Rowntree Mackintosh was born. John Mackintosh & Co. were a renowned toffee and caramel producer; the company, founded in Halifax in 1890 and earned Halifax the soubriquet of 'Toffee Town'. With Mackintosh came classic brands such as Rolo, Munchies, Caramac and the iconic Quality Street.

Chocolate production rolled on through the 1970s with the launch of the 'Yorkie' bar, and production of Kit Kat continued to dominate the '80s. In 1987, the same year that the company went public, corporate advertising asserted that enough Kit Kats were produced every hour to reach the top of the Empire State Building four times over. However, fortune's pendulum swung again, and as the trusts had reduced their stake in the company, Rowntree Mackintosh, then the world's fourth largest confectionery manufacturer, was vulnerable to takeover. In 1988, Nestlé, the Swiss multinational (and largest food company in the world measured by revenues), successfully (and somewhat controversially) outbid fellow Swiss confectionery maker Jacobs Suchard with an offer valuing Rowntree Mackintosh at $4.5 billion.

Renamed Nestlé Rowntree, to become a division of Nestlé UK Ltd, the Haxby Road site, now the York Nestlé factory, continues to produce many of the original branded products, among them the six million Kit Kats produced daily. The Rowntree name lives on in York.

Of course, the universal challenges of commercial competition from domestic and overseas rivals, and the detrimental wartime economics faced by Rowntree, were shared by UK confectionery manufacturers across the board. However, the ultimate outcome for Terry's of York was not so rosy.

The extent of Terry's production and recognition in the marketplace, as mentioned previously, had reached its zenith with the move to expanded premises on Bishopthorpe

The contents of this vintage box of Terry's of York 'Chocolate Assortment' from the 1930s were enjoyed many years ago!

Road in 1927, with peak employment of 2,500 personnel certainly accounting for a considerable portion of York's confectionery industry overall.

Terry's had established their reputation producing a great variety of hard boiled sweets, lozenges (one including opium, harking back to Joseph Terry's apothecary origins), chocolate assortments and a fine, dark, bitter chocolate. They even thoughtfully came up with 'Theatre Chocolates', which came in a rustle-proof wrapper. But with the launch of Terry's 'Chocolate Orange' (born of the 'Dessert Chocolate Apple' introduced in 1924 but withdrawn from production in 1954) and Terry's 'All Gold', both in 1932, the company's already established status as a household name was personified – at one time it was statistically claimed that one in ten Christmas stockings contained a Terry's Chocolate Orange.

It was Francis (Frank) and Noel Terry (sons of Joseph Terry Junior who had opened the steam-powered factory in Clementhorpe) who, having taken over the firm in 1923, would see Terry's through the war years and beyond.

During the Second World War, the Bishopthorpe site was lucky enough to remain unscathed, escaping the fate of Rowntree's North Street warehouse, destroyed in the Baedeker Raid on York on 29 April 1942. In fact, the clock tower of the Terry's factory was utilised as a lookout post for the prisoner of war transit camp based on nearby Knavesmire racecourse. Part of the factory was also given over to the manufacture and repair of Jablo propellers that equipped allied operational fighter aircraft.

In 1941, the company weathered the infamous Edinburgh Poison case, when a jealous Brigadier General called Tredegar (actually a pseudonym, his real name was John Millar) from Edinburgh attempted to poison Georgina Ferguson with a box of Terry's Devon milk chocolates laced with potassium permanganate. After being arrested and duly convicted of attempted murder, 'Tredegar' was sentenced to three years penal servitude, and though Terry's chocolates had been used as the potentially fatal delivery medium, the company's reputation did not ultimately suffer.

After Frank Terry passed away in 1960, rumours of a buyout began rumbling in the York press in early 1961, and though Terry's remained a family concern until 1963, that year the Forte Group bought the company, looking to expand in the chocolate sector. Later passing through various hands (Colgate Palmolive bought Terry in 1978, then sold to United Biscuits in 1982), Terry's was acquired by Kraft in 1993, Kraft in turn merging with Jacobs Suchard to create Terry's Suchard. For the time being, chocolate production remained in York. However, from 2000 onwards, production of the majority of Terry's lines was devolved to Europe, then the final hammer fell in 2004 when Kraft made 6,000 redundancies across all of their operations, Terry's factory doors finally closing in 2005 with the loss of 316 jobs. Today, after the redevelopers and bulldozers have moved in, some of the empty buildings still occupy the Bishopthorpe site, standing as a sad reminder of one of York's premier confectionery concerns, their destiny currently assigned to conversion into a new mixed development of houses, apartments, offices, shops and a hotel.

The final of the triumvirate of major confectionary concerns so integral in the foundation of York as 'Chocolate City', M. A. Craven & Son, were to suffer eclipse much in the same way as Terry's. From auspicious beginnings examined in 'Emergence of 'Chocolate City', by 1908 the M. A. Craven & Son workforce had expanded in number to 800, with production at the site in Coppergate and the additional sites that the company originally held in Coney Street and Foss Island Road, not to mention the four Craven's retail shops dotted around the city. Market leaders in sugared sweets, namely sugared almonds, the original French recipe had been procured by Mary Ann's son after a visit to Paris in 1904, and Craven's 'Original French Almonds' were manufactured in a secure room in order to preserve the secret recipe.

In spite of Craven's many famous brands, among which was 'Mary Ann Dairy Toffee', launched in 1956, the company's fortunes had been in gradual decline since the 1920s.

View of Terry's factory on Bishopthorpe Road, two years after closure.

Right: Advertisement for Craven's 'candies' manufactured at the French Almond Works. (*Courtesy of Grace's Guide*)

Below: York's Chocolate Story, opened in Spring 2012, is now one of York's top themed visitor attractions.

In 1925, Rowntree had approached Craven with a view to them becoming a possible subsidiary, the offer was however declined. By 1936, the company was operating with a diminished workforce of seventy, though Craven's experienced an economic revival with the move to premises on the outskirts of the city in Low Poppleton Lane in 1966, reflected in an increase in staff numbers to 380. But from the late 1980s, Craven were subject to a number of takeovers and mergers, the final buyout taking place in February 2008 by Tangerine Confectionery, the largest UK-owned sugar confectionery and popcorn manufacturer. Today, Tangerine Confectionery continue production from the former Craven's Low Poppleton Road site, and on the back of acquisitions of some of the other household names in confectionery, such as Taveners, Daintee, Parrs, Barratts, Sharps, Jameson's and Trebor Bassett Mints, the company continues to manufacture a range of nostalgic products such as fudge, toffee, pear drops and sherbert, much as Craven's used to more than a century ago.

While the manufacturing heritage of confectionery in York may have suffered an irretrievable eclipse, chocolate is still a dominant presence in the city – and enjoying the history of 'Chocolate City' has never been more accessible, highlighted by the opening of York's own chocolate-themed visitor attraction in the spring of 2012, York's Chocolate Story, in Kings Square in the heart of the city. Offering a fascinating, fully guided tour through the origins of chocolate, and York's most famous chocolate-making families and their finest creations, tutored chocolate tasting is part of the experience, as wel as the opportunity to indulge a sweet tooth in their very own chocolate shop.

VisitYork, part of the country's national tourist board, have even devised a 'chocolate trail', a walking tour highlighting how chocolate has shaped the city, with waypoints at chocolate-themed cafés, chocolate shops and historical sites along the way.

A flavour of the city's chocolate retail past can also be be found in the enduringly popular and faultlessly recreated Victorian Kirkgate, one of the exhibits featured in York Castle Museum. This evocative street scene complete with cobbled road surface and hansom cab includes many shops based on real York businesses that operated between 1870 and 1901, one of which is Terry's sweet shop. Staffed by costumed guides, faithfully schooled in the authenticity of serving customers whose tastes ran from violet lozenges to chocolate worm cakes, a further taste of York's chocolate heritage can be garnered from a worthwhile visit.

York, as you would expect, is a strong participant in national Chocolate Week, which usually takes place in October, a celebration featuring a host of chocolate-themed events, workshops and tastings throughout the city. And since the first York Chocolate Festival took place in April 2012, this event has become an annual occasion held around Easter week, a four-day event focusing on local artisan chocolatiers and showcasing creative ideas and products that chocolate lovers can indulge in around the city. Connoisseur chocolate emporiums can also be found dotted about the city – Monk Bar Chocolatiers, York's longest established artisan chocolatiers, produce handmade chocolates in their evocative premises in The Shambles, while the York Cocoa House, opened in November 2011, offers a shop and café and even a chocolate library and a chocolate school, and for the discerning chocolate shopper, Hotel Chocolat in Coney Street boasts a chocolate selection wide enough to tempt anyone's tastes, from pink champagne to 'egg & chips'.

And for those seeking a truly decadent weekend, a number of York hotels and guest houses now offer a themed 'chocolate break in York'.

It's hard to find an excuse not to share, taste and enjoy York's sweet heritage.

Long Live 'Chocolate City'!